FIVE WEALTH SECRETS 96% OF US DON'T KNOW

BY

CRAIG HILL

FAMILY FOUNDATIONS INTERNATIONAL

LITTLETON, COLORADO

WWW.FAMILYFOUNDATIONS.COM

Family Foundations International
P.O. Box 320
Littleton, Colorado 80160

Printed in the United States of America

All Scripture quotations are taken from The New American
Standard Bible unless otherwise noted: *The New American Standard
Bible*, (NASB), The Lockman Foundation, 1960, 1962, 1963,
1968, 1971, 1973, 1975

The characters in many of the examples cited in this book are real
life people whom the author has known. For their privacy,
however, some names and some of the insignificant details have
been altered. Alternatively, some incidents described are not
sequential events, but are composites of several incidents;
nevertheless, they reflect very real situations.

ACKNOWLEDGEMENTS

My father, Gilman Hill, who taught me many of the principles contained in this book

Jason Dudley for additional graphic design

Chrystal McClung for grammatical editing

DD Tucker for formatting and typesetting

i

ENDORSEMENTS

"Wealth Building 101: God knew that we would all struggle with the basic principles of money, so He put more parables in the New Testament about money than about salvation itself. What Craig has done in this book is simply taken those principles from biblical text and inserted them into the story of how a family, facing the normal financial issues of modern life, utilized them to radically change their lives. And here's the good news. ANYONE, regardless of your current economic status, can immediately begin applying these same principles into your own life and expect success. It's not just the wisdom of God; it's the promise of God!"

Sam Caster, Social Entrepreneur, Founder of Mannatech Inc., and MannaRelief Ministries, Dallas Texas

"Many Jewish people prosper financially because they were raised to follow certain biblical principles. But anyone can prosper — no matter what happens to the economy — when they practice the five wealth principles taught by Craig Hill, one of the best teachers I know."

Sid Roth, Author, Popular Radio and Television Personality, Host of *It's Supernatural!* Television Program and Founder of Messianic Vision

CONTENTS

INTRODUCTION

Many years ago I was impressed when I heard a video presentation by bestselling author, Robert Kiyosaki (Author of Rich Dad, Poor Dad[1]) in which he cited a very interesting statistic. Kiyosaki stated that people tend to use money very differently depending upon their upbringing and financial intelligence. What would be the result a year from now if we were to give 100 people $10,000 today and told them to use the money as they wished? According to Robert Kiyosaki, eighty of the hundred would have $0 left. Sixteen would have about $10,300 to $10,500, or the amount that might be earned by putting the money in the bank at interest. Four would have between $20,000 and $1,000,000 (Two to one hundred times more).

The obvious question then is, "What do the 4% know and practice that the 96% do not?" Kiyosaki goes on to state that the answer has to do with arithmetic functions ingrained in the financial intelligence of each person. Apparently 80% of the people are very good at subtraction; 16% understand something

---

[1] Kiyosaki, Robert T., *Rich Dad Poor Dad* (Paradise Valley AZ TechPress, Inc., 1997)

1

about addition; and only 4% have learned about multiplication. Or in summary:

80%   - (spend)   16%   + (save)   4%   x (multiply)

In this book we will contrast the thinking and practices of the 4% with that of the 96%. While the 16% are somewhat in the middle, and understand some of the first secret that the 4% know, they really have not learned to practice the five secrets of the four percent that lead to wealth generation. In this book we will lump the sixteen percent in with the other eighty percent, and contrast the ninety-six percent with the wealthy four percent. So let's first look at a key understanding that the 4% seem to have.

WISDOM VS. WEALTH

We find that in general **the 4% value knowledge and wisdom above wealth, position, or power.** When Solomon, the son of King David, took the throne in ancient Israel, he expressed to God a very interesting request. The Bible records the following:

2 Chronicles 1:7-12

7 In that night God appeared to Solomon and said to him, "Ask what I shall give you." 8 Solomon said to God, "You have dealt with my father David with great lovingkindness, and have made me king in his place. 9 Now, O LORD God, Your promise to my father David is fulfilled, for You have made me king over a people as numerous as the dust of the earth. 10 Give me now wisdom and knowledge, that I may go out and come in before this people, for who can rule this great people of Yours?" 11 God said to Solomon, "Because you had this in mind, and did not ask for riches, wealth or honor, or the life of those who hate you, nor have you even asked for long life, but you have asked for yourself wisdom and knowledge that you may rule My people over whom I have made you king, 12 wisdom and knowledge have been granted to you. And I will give you riches and wealth and honor, such as none of the kings who were before you has possessed nor those who will come after you.

Here we see Solomon, later known as the wealthiest man on earth in his time, requesting from God wisdom and knowledge, rather than riches, wealth, or honor. I have found this to be common to the 4%. Usually the 96% pursue wealth, power, or position, while the 4% pursue wisdom and knowledge. In actuality, this is what allows the 4% to be granted wealth, position and power. For example, it is a well-known fact that if all wealth were completely removed from one of the 4% thinkers, he/she would have it all back again within just a couple short years. On the other hand, if one of the 96% thinkers were to win a multi-million dollar lottery jackpot, it would likely be all gone within a few short years. Why is this? It is because the 96% thinker does not possess the knowledge or wisdom to retain wealth, and the 4% thinker naturally possesses the knowledge and wisdom to create and retain wealth. Wealth exposes itself to the wise, and is hidden from those who lack wisdom.

A Ukrainian friend of mine shared with me the following account. A very wealthy American friend of his flew in his private transcontinental jet to a Russian city to observe and consider supporting the Christian ministry in which my friend was involved. While there, my friend arranged a meeting for the wealthy American with several would-be Russian entrepreneurs from that city. Each of these businessmen came with a hope that the wealthy American would take an interest in their particular business and provide funding for it.

However, one Russian businessman came with no agenda for funding, but only a desire to learn and access the wisdom of the wealthy American. When the wealthy businessman asked each of the would-be entrepreneurs what was hindering them from growing their respective businesses, they each in turn expressed that it was a lack of funding that was holding them back. Only the one man expressed that it was a lack of wisdom that was restraining him. He was convinced that God would release plenty of funding to expand his business when he had obtained the character and wisdom necessary to manage the funds and the expanded business. He told the wealthy American, "I don't need your money. I need your wisdom and counsel." This attitude so impressed the wealthy American businessman that he chose to mentor this one Russian man, imparting to him his wisdom and experience. However, he chose not to provide funding for any of them.

> "I don't need your money. I need your wisdom and counsel."

Several years have now passed since this initial visit of the wealthy American businessman. I asked my friend what had occurred in the businesses of each of the entrepreneurs who attended that first meeting. My friend told me that the man who sought wisdom is now running a rapidly growing multi-million dollar business that has expanded to several cities in Russia. Each of the other businessmen are still "waiting for funding" to get started in their businesses. So what do you need to move forward in your business or financial life: more wisdom and character, or more money?

WISDOM ENTAILS BOTH SPIRIT AND TRUTH

Another friend of mine, Earl Pitts, told me of an interesting conversation he had with his Jewish accountant many years ago. After discussing his taxes, Earl queried if he might ask the man a personal question. The accountant was happy to oblige him.

Earl then asked, "I assume that you have both Jewish and Christian clients. Am I right?"

"Of course," answered the accountant.

"Tell me honestly, continued Earl, "Who is more prosperous? Who has larger financial statements; your Jewish clients, or your Christian clients?"

As one might suspect, the accountant chuckled and responded, "My Jewish clients, of course. Probably about ten to one in magnitude."

Earl then asked, "One more question. Being Jewish yourself, what is your personal opinion as to why that is?"

The accountant mused for a moment, then picked up Earl's Christian Bible, which he had with him and said something like the following: "You Christians tend to live out of the back of this book, while we Jews tend to live out of the front of the book. Unfortunately for Christians, most of the financial principles are in the front of the book. So we Jews believe in and abide by these principles, while you Christians seem to ignore them and discount them because they are 'Old Testament.' However, I believe that the adherence to these principles is what causes people to prosper financially."

Since I first heard this from my friend Earl, I have heard several times from Jewish friends explanations similar to the following: "I don't really fully understand your Christian beliefs, but from what I understand, it seems that most Christians have the idea that they can violate the basic principles described in the Bible, and then because of the grace of God extended by the sacrifice of Christ, they are forgiven, and everything will be alright. Thus it seems to me that most Christians feel that they don't have to pay any attention to the financial principles explained in Proverbs, or the rest of the 'Old Testament' because these are a part of 'the Law.' Since Christians are 'in Christ,' and no longer 'under the law,' they feel no need to abide by these Old Testament financial principles. On the contrary, we Jews believe that we actually have to practice and abide by these principles in the Law. So, in my opinion and experience, abiding by the biblical financial principles produces much greater financial prosperity than ignoring and discounting them."

My personal observation has been that many Evangelical and Charismatic Christians like to study the Bible. Many can tell you exactly where in the Bible a particular passage is located and even quote the verse to you. However, frequently, while they have studied the Bible passage, such Christians have in practice violated the life principle contained in the passage. On the other hand, many Jewish people cannot tell you where in the Bible a particular passage is, but because of culture and the teaching of their family, they inherently practice the principle.

For example, Proverbs 22:7 tells us that the borrower is slave to the lender. It may be common in our day for a Jewish banker to be the mortgage holder (lender) on the home of a Bible-believing Christian (borrower) who holds a weekly Bible study group in his home regarding Biblical principles of finance. The Christian mortgagee can tell you all about where to find passages in the Bible about debt, while the Jewish banker may not know where in the Bible to find these passages. Yet who is the master and who is the slave? Who is making money, and who is spending money? In reality, the Jewish lender has chosen to be the master, while the Christian borrower has chosen to be the slave. So which is better: to study the Bible and not live out the principles contained therein, or to live out the principles and not study the Bible? I would suggest that we do both, study <u>and</u> live out the principles.

In this book, we will endeavor to keep a balance between "spirit and truth," for therein lies wisdom.

Jesus told us in

John 4:23

23 But an hour is coming, and now is, when the true worshipers will worship the Father in spirit and truth; for such people the Father seeks to be His worshipers.

What does it mean to worship in spirit and truth? I believe that it means the following. There are basic immutable principles that govern all areas of life on planet earth. In the physical realm, gravity would be such a principle. Gravity affects everyone everywhere and yields a consequence for its violation. This is what I call a "truth principle." On the other hand, we also understand that God designed us to be in relationship with Him, and to expect to experience supernatural miracles in our lives. Miracles tend to operate by faith. Expectation of, and faith for miracles would be a "spirit principle."

So, suppose you are presented with two options to ride in a car over a high mountain pass on a very narrow, windy road. One option entails riding in a car with a driver who has had many car accidents, has no regard for speed limits, automobile maintenance, or gravity, but is a great man of faith, who hears from God, has incredible spiritual discernment, and frequently experiences miracles in his life. The second option entails riding with a driver who does not know God, is not a spiritual man, has no faith, doesn't believe in miracles, but is a very careful driver, has had no past car accidents, who diligently maintains his car, and follows the speed limits.

With which driver would you prefer ride? I think most of us would like to choose a third alternative. You might say, "Could I please have a driver who is a spiritual man of faith, but also abides by the "truth" principles of safe automobile operation, and is an experienced mountain driver?" So when it comes to finances, we need to learn how to walk in a balance of both spirit and truth.

FIVE WEALTH SECRETS THAT 96% OF US DON'T KNOW

In the succeeding chapters, we will discuss five very simple "truth" principles of wisdom that the 4% seem to naturally understand and practice, and the 96% seem not to know. I call these "secrets" not because they are unknowable, but rather because they generally are unknown by most people. These five secrets are clearly explained in the Bible to those who have eyes to see them. Perhaps you have had a general understanding of these principles, but have not fully embraced or practiced them. Or perhaps no one ever took the time to clearly explain these simple principles to you. In the succeeding chapters, we will clearly examine these five secrets of wisdom that anyone can implement and practice. As we start, let's look at an overview of the five secrets.

1. The 4% segregate their money into several distinct categories of use (jars) and intentionally prioritize their usage.

2. The 4% focus their life on fulfilling a calling and vision.

3. The 4% invest their resources only in things that multiply. They also invest their time and energy in people who multiply.

4. The 4% understand that the economy flows in cycles, and therefore they anticipate and prepare for each new phase in the cycle.

5. The 4% prepare for and leave an inheritance for at least two subsequent generations.

Below is a chart contrasting the thinking and practice of the 4% as opposed to the 96%.

PRINCIPLE	4%	96%
1. Manage Money in -	Five Jars	One Jar
2. Focus on -	Vision	Provision
3. Invest in -	Things that Multiply and Never Pay Interest (Use No Personal Debt)	Things that Depreciate and Pay Lots of Interest (Use Much Personal Debt)
4. Anticipate and Prepare for -	Cyclical Economy	Linear Economy
5. Leave an Inheritance for -	Two Generations	No Future Generations

CHAPTER 1

USE JARS

Let's look at the first secret the 4% understand and regularly practice. This has to do with how money is stored and used. The 4% and the 96% use money entirely differently. The 96% focus on what they earn, while the 4% focus on how they use what they earn. If you ask the 96% what their financial problem is, they will usually tell you that they don't make enough money, and their necessary expenses are too high. They will say, "The boss doesn't pay me what I'm worth. The landlord charges too much rent for the house. The price of gasoline is way too high, and the government takes way too much in taxes." The 4% will simply tell you "I'm working on building my cash flow, and my plan is in process."

> The 96% focus on what they earn, while the 4% focus on how they use what they earn.

The 96% believe that rich or poor is defined by how much money someone receives. They think the rich are defined as people who make a lot of money each month, or have a lot of available resources. The poor are defined by the 96% as people who don't make much money each month and have very little available resources. On the other hand, the 4% define the rich as people who voluntarily limit their spending and choose to invest in things that multiply. The poor are defined by the 4% as people who spend 100% or more of all the money they make each month. Thus, while the 96% define rich or poor by the quantity of their income, the 4% define rich or poor by the usage of their income. To the 4%, it doesn't matter how much the income is because they know how to multiply the allocated percentage of any amount of available income.

So, as an example the 96% thinker who makes $4,000 per month will take on monthly expenses of $4,000 (or a little more) and will constantly be pressured to make ends meet, desperately working overtime and looking for a second job to increase his income to $5,000 per month. The 4% thinker who makes only $2,000 per month will limit his monthly expenses to $1,400 per month and will invest $300 per month in a vision or assets that multiply. Within a few years, the $300 per month of the 4% thinker will have multiplied to $30,000 per month, while the 96% thinker may have increased his income to $5,000 per month, but will likewise have increased his monthly expenses to $5,000 per month or more, and will still be under the same financial pressure as before.

What's the difference in storage and usage of money between the 4% and the 96%? The 4% store their money in multiple receptacles, while the 96% usually store their money in just one receptacle. The 4% tend to give, save and invest first, and spend what's left, while the 96% tend to spend first and then try to give, save and invest what's left. While the 4% always have a specified percentage left to spend, the 96% usually have nothing left to give, save, or invest. This is not because the 4% necessarily have more money to start with. They simply choose to use the money they have differently. Throughout the remainder of the book, I would like to illustrate these five secrets with a story about a boy named Isaac and the wisdom imparted to him from his father.

Isaac had just turned ten years old and his father had decided to begin to teach him about handling money. So Isaac's dad met with him one day and declared,

"Isaac, starting this week, each Sunday I'm going to give you an allowance of $10. You can use this $10 any way you like, but I'd like to share with you some ideas that I think will help you in your life as you continue to grow up. Ancient wisdom from our fathers tells us that *"The rich rules over the poor, and the borrower becomes slave to the lender"* (Proverbs 22:7). Son, when you grow up, which would you rather be, rich or poor? Would you rather be a master, or a slave?

"Hmmm," Isaac pondered, "Rich – poor? Master – slave?" "Papa, I think I'd rather be rich, and be a master."

"Good choice," remarked the father. Now let me ask you a question about your first ten dollars. Here it is. What would you like to do with it?"

"Wow!" exclaimed Isaac. "You mean I can do anything I want with it."

"That's right," his father replied.

"I'm going to buy a candy bar, and a couple of new games for my iphone," exclaimed Isaac.

"How much will that cost you?" asked his father?

Adding it up in his head, "Exactly ten dollars," said Isaac.

"Son, you just qualified yourself to be a poor person," declared Isaac's father.

"A poor person is someone who spends 100% of the dollar. Ninety-six percent of the people will normally make the choice to spend 100% of the money they receive. Only four percent will spend less than 100% of their money. Son, let's get in the car and go for a drive."

Isaac's father drove him to one of the slum areas of their city. They drove up and down a couple of streets lined by houses with weeds growing up all over the yard, trash littered all around, windows of some houses boarded up due to broken glass, and old dilapidated automobiles, which no longer ran, sitting in some driveways. Most houses were in desperate need of paint.

Pointing at one brown wooden house with the front screen door falling off the hinges, Isaac's father asked him, "Son, would you like to live in that house when you grow up?"

"No Papa," Isaac grimaced.

"Do you know who lives in that house, Isaac?"

"No, who Papa?" inquired Isaac.

"Someone who spends 100% of the dollars they make, and puts all of their money in one jar. Someone who is in debt and is a slave to others who control his life is the one who lives here."

"How about that one?" pointing to another dilapidated house across the street from the first. "Would you like to live there?"

"No Papa. I wouldn't like to live in any of the houses in this neighborhood," remarked Isaac.

"Do you know who lives in that house, Isaac?"

"Maybe someone who spends 100% of the money they make?" answered Isaac.

"Right," said his father. "You're learning."

Isaac's father then drove to a gated community in which two of Isaac's uncles lived. He drove down an unfamiliar street in the community and stopped in front of one of the large homes, with a beautifully manicured lawn and a 5-car garage, and a swimming pool in the back yard.

Isaac, would you like to live in that house?

"Wow! Yes, Papa. I would love to live in that house."

"Son, do you know who lives in that house?" asked his father.

"No," responded Isaac.

"Someone who has limited his spending to much less than 100% of the dollar and has kept his money in several different jars," replied Papa. "Actually the man who owns this house is a friend of mine. His name is Mr. Tran, and he has not always lived here. About fifteen years ago he and his family emigrated from Vietnam. He was looking for a better life, and had a dream in his heart to start a business here in America."

"Before he left Vietnam, Mr. Tran had done extensive development work on a new software program he hoped to use to start his business. According to his research, Mr. Tran had determined that he needed about fifty thousand dollars to start his business. After settling into his one room apartment with his wife and three children, Mr. Tran approached several local banks in hopes of getting a loan to start his new business. However, because he spoke very little English, had no prior credit history, and was a new immigrant, he found that no bank was willing to lend him any money."

"Initially Mr. Tran was very discouraged," continued Papa. "However, sitting down with his family, he designed a plan to save the necessary fifty thousand dollars over a period of four years. Mr. Tran discovered that he and his family could make a net income of about two thousand five hundred dollars per month selling fruit and vegetables from a mobile stand in the street. Because Mr. Tran understood the importance of putting his money in jars, his family was able to limit their spending and put a little over one thousand dollars per month, or about twelve thousand five hundred dollars per year in their savings jar. They did this by living in a one-bedroom apartment, not owning a car, never eating in restaurants, and avoiding any other unnecessary expenses."

"Through consistently putting their money in jars, Mr. Tran was able to save the necessary fifty thousand dollars in just over four years. By that time, he had learned to speak English well and was ready to start his business. It turned out, Isaac," continued Papa, "that Mr. Tran had developed cutting edge software applicable to mobile devices before anyone else knew how to do it. Needless to say, that has become a huge business now. His company grew very rapidly, and within three of four years, the fifty thousand dollars he had saved to invest in his business had multiplied into a two or three million dollar annual profit for Mr. Tran personally. I suspect that it has grown even larger now."

"Isaac," asked Papa, "if you would have seen Mr. Tran fifteen years ago selling fruit from his stand on the street, with no car, and a family of five living in a one bedroom apartment, would you have thought him to be a rich or poor person?"

"I would have thought that he was a poor person, Papa," replied Isaac.

"Indeed, that is how it looked. But you see, Isaac," continued Papa, "whether someone is rich or poor depends on how they think and behave, not on what they have at the moment. It turned out that Mr. Tran was one of the 4% thinkers, who was willing to limit his spending, and put his money in more than one jar in order to fulfill a vision in his heart. For the first four years of his life in America, the vision God had given Mr. Tran was like a seed in the ground that had not yet germinated. When that seed sprouted, it grew into a tall tree very quickly. If you look at this house where Mr. Tran and his family live now, you can see the fruit of his vision and the way he managed his money in jars when he first came here."

"When Mr. Tran arrived in this country, he had very little choice about how much money was available to him. The maximum he could earn was twenty-five hundred dollars per month. However, he did have a choice about how he used the money he made. Mr. Tran chose to use the money very differently than most other people who only make twenty-five hundred dollars per month to care for a family of five. Ninety-six percent of the other people would spend the entire amount they made, and frequently complain that they don't make enough money to support a family of five. Mr. Tran made a different choice.

"Do you understand now, Isaac, what makes someone rich and what makes someone poor?" asked his father.

"Yes, Papa," replied Isaac. "It depends on how people use the money they have, not on how much money they have now, right?"

"Exactly," said Papa. "Let's go home and talk more about how you might use the ten dollars you will have each week."

Upon arriving home, they once again sat down at the kitchen table and Isaac asked, "Okay, Papa. I understand now that it would not be wise for me to spend all of my ten dollars this week. So how should I divide my money, and how should I manage it?"

"Just a minute and I'll show you," said Papa, getting up and disappearing from the kitchen. A few moments later he returned with five empty peanut butter jars. On each jar was a taped label. Papa got out ten one dollar bills and handed them to Isaac. He then began to explain.

"Son, as I told you, ninety-six percent of the people will put all their money in only one jar. They will spend everything in the jar, thus qualifying themselves to be poor. Only four percent of the people will put their money in several jars and never move the money between jars. So, as you have already seen, the first secret to become rich and a master, instead of poor and a slave, is to make sure that you never spend 100% of your money. You do this by dividing the money you receive into physically separate jars and never moving it between jars."

"So let's look at the five jars we have. As you can see that the label on this first jar says, 'The Lord's Tithe.' God told our fathers many years ago that 10% of everything we receive belongs to Him (Leviticus 27:30). The word that means 10% of your income belongs to God is the word 'tithe.' So, this 10%, the tithe, is a qualification test to see if you know how to handle money that doesn't belong to you."

"This is not your money that you give to God, but rather it is God's money He lets you administrate as a qualification test, to see if you recognize what is His and not yours. If you faithfully deliver God's money to His congregation, to be used for His purpose, then God will release much more money for you to use to fulfill the calling and vision He has given you. God is very smart. He gives each person a small amount of His money to manage, called 'The Lord's Tithe' to see who is qualified to manage a much larger amount of His money."

"So, I suggest that you take one dollar, ten percent of your ten dollars, and place it in 'The Lord's Tithe' jar each week. You deliver all the money in this jar to the congregation each week. A mistake that most poor people make is that they mix 'The Lord's Tithe' in with the money they use for spending and paying their bills. Because they have deposited the whole ten dollars in only one jar, they get confused and spend all the money including 'The Lord's Tithe'. God still loves them, but they have disqualified themselves from ever having much of their own money because they have not learned how to manage what belongs to someone else (Luke 16:12). So let's put one dollar in 'The Lord's Tithe' jar.

"Okay Papa," said Isaac taking one of the crisp new dollar bills and placing it in the first jar.

"This second jar is labeled 'Offerings.' We always want to have some money available to give to people who need mercy, who have experienced tragedy or are victims of disaster. God loves people, and we want to have some money available to help others in need. So let's take another dollar and put it in the 'Offerings' jar."

Isaac took another dollar and places it in this second jar.

Isaac's father continued. "This third jar is labeled 'Savings.' Let's take another dollar and store it in this jar to save for larger purchases of things you may wish to buy. The money in this jar can also be used for unexpected expenses in the future."

Isaac placed another dollar in this third jar.

"This fourth jar is labeled, 'Investing.' Let's place two dollars in this jar," said Papa.

Isaac followed his father's instructions and placed two dollars in this fourth jar.

"And of course, this fifth jar is labeled, 'Spending.'" You can use the money in this jar to purchase the things you need and want. How many dollars do you have left, Isaac?"

"Five dollars, Papa. Should I put them all in the 'Spending' jar?"

"Yes, Isaac. Let's put the remaining five dollars in the 'Spending' jar," replied Papa.

Isaac then looked a little puzzled and remarked, "Papa, I understand how to use money in 'The Lord's Tithe' jar, the 'Offerings' jar, the 'Savings' jar, and I for sure understand the 'Spending' jar. But what is investing?"

"Well son," replied Papa, "investing is placing your money somewhere that will increase its value, usually through producing a product or performing a valuable service for others. You are then paid by those who buy your product, or receive your service more than it cost you to produce the product or perform the service. This increased amount is called a profit and causes the money in your Investment jar to grow larger and larger. Let me ask you a question. Do any of the other kids at your school receive an allowance from their fathers?"

"Yes, Papa. I think lots of them do."

"Probably most of their fathers have not taught their sons the ancient wisdom I am teaching you. So most of the kids at school will spend 100% of the money they have each week. Then long about Thursday or Friday they will be asking if anyone will lend them money for the weekend. They will promise to repay the money on Monday after they receive their allowance again, and they will offer to give you back much more than you lent them. By lending them the money they request, you will be providing a valuable service to your schoolmates, for which they will pay you a profit.

Don't tell the kids who want to borrow how much extra you want them to give you back. Just allow them to offer what they are willing to pay you for the use of the money you lend them over the weekend. They will set their own interest rate. This will be your first lesson in providing a service for people, for which they are willing to pay you a profit. This is called investing."

"Okay," said Isaac. "I'll wait and see what happens this week at school."

So the next Friday, sure enough, Billy began asking at recess if anyone had any money to lend him. He said he just needed two dollars to go to a movie he desperately wanted to see over the weekend, and that he would give back four dollars on Monday after he received his next allowance from his dad.

Isaac got out his two dollars that he brought to school that day from his 'Investing' jar and gave it to Billy. At home, he later asked his father why Billy would be willing to give him back four dollars, or 100% interest for only three days' use of the money. Papa explained that most people, who have unwittingly made the choice to become slaves of others, think and behave in this manner.

"It is illogical," he said, "but nonetheless, this is how 96% of the people think." Isaac was baffled, but at the same time excited at the prospect of multiplying his money.

On Monday, sure enough, Billy returned with the four dollars and was very grateful to Isaac for having lent him the money. Isaac waited to see what would happen at the end of the next week. By Thursday Billy had told two of his friends, Bobby and Jimmy. They each asked Isaac if he had any more money to lend over the weekend. Isaac, of course, had four dollars from before and another two dollars from his dad's allowance in his 'Investing' jar. So he brought the six dollars to school on Friday and lent two dollars to each of the three other boys. Billy had once again spent all of his money and had forgotten about something he really needed money for over the weekend. Each of the boys who borrowed money from Isaac offered to pay him back double the next Monday.

The following Monday, Isaac received twelve dollars from the three boys and had another two dollars from his father for a total of fourteen dollars in his Investing jar. Word began to spread through the school that if you needed to borrow money, Isaac usually could help you. So the third week Isaac lent his fourteen dollars and received back on Monday twenty-eight dollars and another two dollars from his allowance. Continuing to "invest" his money with the other students at his school, Isaac's money grew quickly over the weeks according to the following schedule.

Week 1: $2 \times 2 = 4 + 2 = \$6$

Week 2: $6 \times 2 = 12 + 2 = \$14$

Week 3: $14 \times 2 = 28 + 2 = \$30$

Week 4: $30 \times 2 = 60 + 2 = \$62$

Week 5: $124 + 2 = \$126$

Week 6: $252 + 2 = \$254$

Week 7: $508 + 2 = \$510$

Week 8: $1020 + 2 = \$1022$

Isaac was absolutely shocked that after only a few months, the amount of money in his 'Investment' jar had grown to over $1000. He asked his father, "Papa, I don't understand why the other the kids at school don't do the same as I am doing. All of the other kids who borrow money from me each week receive an allowance from their fathers. Some of them receive $15 or $20 per week, which is much more than the $10 I receive. Why do they spend it all each week and then request to borrow more from me?"

"Good question, Isaac," said Papa. "You see, everyone has a choice about how they use their money. Most people don't have a choice about how much money they receive. Neither you nor the other kids at school get to choose how much allowance you receive from your parents. That is the choice of the parents. Each child only has a choice about how he uses the money he receives. But if you were to ask the other kids in your school how they could have more money, they would each tell you that in order to have more money they would have to convince their parents to give them a bigger allowance."

Papa continued, "All of the kids at your school have the same opportunity you do to multiply money. The reason they don't do so is firstly they don't use jars, and instead simply put all their money in one jar. You see, human nature dictates that we will spend 100% of whatever is in our 'Spending' jar. If you only have one jar for your money, then you will spend all the money that is in that jar.

> You see, human nature dictates that we will spend 100% of whatever is in our 'Spending' jar.

Secondly, most kids think that the way to increase wealth is to focus on getting more money from their parents. In reality, only 4% of the people understand that the secret to becoming wealthy is in how you use the money you have, not in getting more money from your parents. So the first secret is to limit your spending by allocating percentages of your money into various jars that are designated for various purposes, and not moving the money from one jar to another."

When summer came and school was out, Isaac once again pursued making a little money by mowing his neighbors' lawns, as he had the previous summer. Because Isaac was a very diligent and meticulous worker, he soon had more neighbors requesting his services than he had time available to work. An idea occurred to Isaac. "Perhaps," he thought, "I could use some of the money I have made through the school year to purchase another lawnmower and employ Billy, who is also a very diligent worker, to mow the lawns I don't have time to get to."

Isaac checked with Billy, who was thrilled to be able to earn some extra money. So Isaac decided to ask his father to see what he thought about this idea. Papa seemed very pleased at this idea and told Isaac to go ahead and use some of the money he had accumulated in his 'Investment' jar to purchase another lawnmower. This would be his second lesson in learning how to invest.

Isaac normally charged twenty dollars to mow an average-sized lawn in his neighborhood. He told Billy, "I'll pay you twelve dollars for each of the lawns I give you to mow."

"Yah, but you are charging the neighbor twenty dollars and only paying me twelve. Why?" asked Billy.

"Simple said Isaac. I need pay for the lawnmower, the maintenance, gas and oil and the time it took me to find the customer and make a deal to mow his lawn. Then I need to make a small profit as well. However, I'll tell you what," offered Isaac. "If you find a new customer, I'll give you two dollars more each time you mow his lawn."

"Okay," said Billy. "I understand. That's fair."

So Isaac bought a second lawn mower and he and Billy mowed lawns. Billy found two additional customers and was able to make a little more money himself on each of those lawns.

Six weeks into the summer, because word of mouth had spread, Isaac found that again, he and Billy had more lawns to mow than time available. Isaac didn't want to mow lawns all day every day. So he contacted Bobby and Jacob to see if they would like to mow lawns too, on the same basis upon which he had hired Billy. They both expressed an interest. So Isaac bought two more lawnmowers. He also used a little money from his 'Investment' jar and bought a small advertisement in the local community newspaper.

Isaac's lawn mowing business prospered and grew all summer. Isaac worried that perhaps Billy would save enough money to buy his own lawnmower and start his own business to compete with Isaac. However, Billy continued to spend all the money he made each week, and sometimes even borrowed more money from Isaac over the weekends, so this turned out to be an unfounded fear.

The next summer, a few weeks before school got out, Isaac purchased a larger ad in the local community newspaper for his lawn mowing business. Based on the response, it was evident that Isaac was going to need more workers. He was also a little concerned about Jacob, who had saved some money and perhaps could buy his own lawn mower. Isaac thought that maybe he should ask his father for his wisdom on these matters.

"Hi Papa," said Isaac as he came into his father's study. "Can I ask a couple of questions about my lawn business?"

"Sure," replied Papa. "Go ahead. "

"Well," started Isaac, "I'm afraid that Jacob may buy his own lawn mower and start his own business to compete with me. Also, I already have more work than we can handle this summer. What do you think I should do?"

"Hmmm," mused Papa, taking a sip of his iced tea. "Well Son, in order to keep Jacob, you will need to offer him the same opportunity you have to hire his own workers and to earn a profit from their work. Otherwise he will start his own business and become your competitor."

"So, I would suggest that you increase your price this year by one dollar, to twenty-one dollars per average lawn. Then offer Jacob the opportunity to buy his own lawnmower and to earn eighteen dollars per lawn you give him to mow. If Jacob buys more lawn mowers and hires his own workers, you can then offer him the opportunity to still benefit from your advertising and the good name you have created for the business over the last couple of years. He won't have to do his own advertising and build a business from scratch, and you will only ask him to pay you three dollars for each lawn his crew mows. For each lawn, he can then pay his workers twelve dollars, as you do, pay you three dollars, and still make six dollars per lawn for his own overhead and profit."

"That's brilliant, Papa," exclaimed Isaac. "That way Jacob will want to continue working with me, rather than start his own business and take away some of my customers."

The next day Isaac approached Jacob with the offer Papa had suggested. Jacob thought about the proposal for a few minutes and ran some simple calculations on his calculator. He then turned to Isaac and announced, "Okay Isaac. You've got a deal."

That summer Isaac's lawn care business exploded as he increased his advertising and spent more of his time riding his bike around the neighborhood passing out the advertising brochures Papa had helped him make. By the end of the summer, Isaac had hired two more workers and had very little time to mow lawns himself, as most of his time was taken up acquiring new customers, maintaining his lawnmowers and scheduling the jobs his friends, who worked for him, were to complete each day. Meanwhile, Jacob had diligently increased the number of customers in another neighborhood near where he lived.

Over the next several years, each summer, Isaac's lawn care business continued to grow. The following summer Simon, who had started to work for Isaac the previous summer also wanted to buy his own lawnmowers and start the business in another neighborhood as Jacob had done the previous year. Isaac offered Simon the same deal as he had given to Jacob. Simon's part of the business in the new neighborhood also began to rapidly grow.

Meanwhile, through middle school and high school, during the school year, Isaac continued to lend money to other students in his school. Of course he was not able to continue to double his money each week, but he was able to continually increase the amount of money in his 'Investment' jar. By the time he was in eighth grade, students from other schools began contacting Isaac to borrow money from him as well. Even before this, Isaac had far too much money to keep at home in his jars. So his father took him to the bank and suggested that Isaac open five separate bank accounts and use the accounts exactly the same as he had been using the physical jars at home, which he did.

During his sophomore year in high school, news of Isaac's willingness to lend money had spread far and wide. Actually, Billy's parents approached Isaac and asked if he would be willing to lend them money to buy a new big screen TV. Isaac agreed to do so at a more favorable rate than the department store was offering. Soon this news spread and Bobby's parents, Jimmy's older married brother, and several other families also approached Isaac to finance various household appliances they wished to purchase. Isaac quickly consulted his father as to how to handle these new opportunities to finance purchases made by adults. Isaac realized that this was turning into a real business, which required a legal structure and appropriate accounting and management.

Isaac's father suggested that Isaac meet with his attorney to help him create a Limited Liability Company (LLC) to house this business, and to draft legal financing agreements to aid in lending money to the parents of his schoolmates. Papa also took Isaac to see his accountant to help establish the financing terms for his friends' parents, and to obtain some counsel on how to manage the significant tax liability that he was now incurring. The accountant suggested that Isaac purchase a couple of smaller houses to rent to others and reduce his taxes by writing off the interest paid for the houses. In addition, Isaac would increase his monthly cash flow and gain equity in the houses, since the real estate market in his city was inflating every year. Isaac followed the accountant's advice, and with his father's help was able to finance the houses based on his own net worth, and his father's guarantee.

Now that Isaac's monthly cash flow had become significant, his father suggested that they meet and talk a little more about Isaac's jars.

Papa started out, "Isaac, you have been faithful to allocate your money into each of the five jars every month. But I have noticed that the actual amount in just your spending account (jar) is more than many adults make in total each month. Money is only a tool to be used to accomplish a purpose. Personal consumption has value, but not great purpose. As you graduate from high school, you will need money to accomplish your calling and purpose in your adult life. What do you think you might want to use money for after high school?"

"Well," Isaac pondered. "I think I'd like to get married. I'd like to own a home. I think that my primary calling is probably to be a businessman. So I think I'll need some money to start one or two businesses."

"Excellent thinking, son," remarked Papa. I suggest then that you reallocate the percentages in your jars, as your situation in life is changing. I suggest that you now reduce the percentage in your 'Spending' jar from 50% to 25% and increase the amount in your 'Offering' jar to 15%, your 'Savings' jar to 20% and your 'Investing' jar to 30%."

Isaac agreed to further limit his spending during the rest of high school and to increase the percentages in his other jars, as his father had suggested. By the time Isaac graduated from high school, at the suggestion of his accountant and his father, he used money from his 'Investment' jar to purchase in addition to the two houses, two small apartment complexes and a self-service car wash. Isaac did not purchase these businesses for cash, but rather used financing from the bank, since the economy was in a significant inflation cycle at that time.

One evening in May of his senior year in high school, Papa asked Isaac at dinner if he could speak with him briefly that evening about his lawn care business. Isaac willingly agreed.

"So Papa," said Isaac, as Papa sat down in his favorite chair in the living room. "What are you thinking?"

"Well Isaac," started Papa, "I was just wondering what your plans were for that business. It has grown quite large with four other guys like Jacob and Simon running their own 'franchises' as it were, and twenty people, in total, mowing lawns."

"I don't know," answered Isaac. "I hadn't really thought about it."

"Do you really want to continue each summer doing all the work it takes to manage that business? Last summer, it seems to me that the business growth has slowed down and become pretty flat. However, your business creates a very reliable, stable cash flow, and would be a great investment for someone who wants to pour his primary time and energy into lawn care. I am thinking that now may be a great time to sell the business, since you are graduating, and I don't think that this is the field into which you may want to pour your primary time and energy long-term."

"Wow," exclaimed Isaac, "I hadn't thought of that. How much do you think I could get for the business, Papa?"

"I'm not sure," replied Papa, "but you may want to ask for some cash up front and let the buyer pay the rest over a few years out of the cash flow from the business. Most people could not afford to pay the full value of the business up front."

"That's a great idea," said Isaac excitedly. "I think I will try to sell the business."

"Let's go talk to the accountant," suggested Papa. "He can help us calculate the net present worth of the future cash flow from the business and determine a present value. That should give us some idea what to ask for it."

Isaac and his father met the accountant, determined a price, and listed the lawn care business for sale. By mid July, with Papa's counsel, Isaac had negotiated a sale with a man who had just moved to town from Florida. He had sold a business there, and had been thinking of starting a new lawn care business, a field for which he had a love and some experience.

When he ran across Isaac's business for sale, the potential buyer determined that he would much rather purchase an established business than go through all the difficulty of starting a new one. Even better yet, because he had sold a prior business in Florida, the buyer was willing and able to purchase Isaac's business for cash up front. Negotiating a slightly discounted price for the cash sale, the buyer closed the deal and took ownership of his new lawn care business in early August, a couple months after Isaac had graduated from high school.

Allocating the proceeds from the sale into his five jars by predetermined percentages, Isaac promptly divided this large sum of money and deposited it directly into the bank accounts corresponding with each jar. Even though Isaac had enough money in his spending and savings jar to purchase a brand new car, he chose to limit his spending to purchase a one-year old Honda Civic for cash from his 'Savings' jar. At twenty-one years of age, Isaac married Rachael, the love of his life, and purchased his first home to live in for cash, using proceeds of the sale of his lawn care business, supplemented by money, which he had accumulated in his Savings jar.

Meanwhile, Billy, Bobby and Jimmy also graduated from the same high school as Isaac. One day during his junior year in high school, Billy received in the mail an offer for a credit card. The annual fee was even waived for the first year. In order to sign up for the Master Card offer, Billy's father had to guarantee the account, which he willingly did. By the time he graduated from high school, Billy had already accumulated a credit card balance of $2,500. Billy had told Bobby and Jimmy and they each had gotten their parents to help them obtain a credit card too, and had run up a balance on their cards. All three boys purchased brand new turbo-charged sports cars after graduation and financed them through the dealership. Billy, Bobby, and Jimmy all struggled each month in their young adult lives to earn enough money to pay their apartment rent, car payment, and credit card minimum payments.

What was the difference between the learning experience of Isaac growing up, and that of his three friends, Billy, Bobby, and Jimmy? Because of the ancient wisdom from his father, Isaac learned to put his money in jars and to give, save and invest first. He thereby learned to be rich and to be a master over others to whom he lent. The other three boys actually received a larger weekly allowance from their parents, but they each put all their money in only one jar and spent it all each week. They then found themselves in need of borrowing more money at the end of most weeks to meet their desires and obligations. So Billy, Bobby, and Jimmy learned to spend and borrow, thereby qualifying themselves to be poor and slaves to lenders. These patterns then continued on into the adult lives of all four young men.

Secret Number 1: Place your money in five jars and allocate a percentage to each jar. Voluntarily limit your spending to the percentage allocated to the 'Spending' jar, and never rob the money in one jar to fund an activity in another jar (especially the 'Spending' jar).

Reflection

1. What is your experience of using one jar or multiple jars for your finances?

2. What have you learned from your parents growing up regarding the management of money through multiple jars or just one jar?

    a. How did your parents manage their money?

    b. How did they teach you to manage money?

3. Do you know someone like Mr. Tran, described in this chapter, who has prospered through using jars?

4. In what ways would you be willing to limit your spending as Mr. Tran did in order to fulfill a future vision for your life?

5. What is your plan going forward to implement the concept of using jars with your finances?

   a. What percentages do you think would be
      reasonable for you to use for each of the five jars?

6. If you have children, what is your plan to teach your children
   how to manage their money in jars?

CHAPTER 2

FOCUS ON VISION

Now let's turn to the second secret the 96% don't understand or practice. While the 96% tend to focus on provision, the 4% focus on VISION. When you ask most people why they cannot accomplish a goal, they will tell you that the prevailing reason is they don't have the money to do so. The focus of these people is on provision, rather than on vision. The 4% believe that provision naturally follows vision. Thus they choose to focus on establishing clear vision with an expectation that provision will naturally follow.

> While the 96% tend to focus on provision, the 4% focus on VISION.

In the summer after graduation from high school, Isaac went with his whole family on a tourist trip to Israel. While on a boat ride on the Sea of Galilee, Isaac and his whole family had a dramatic encounter with God. Through his interaction with a group of Messianic Jewish believers on the boat, Isaac and his family came to recognize Yeshua (Jesus) as the promised Jewish Messiah.

Upon returning home, Isaac became very involved in a local church congregation to which many other Jewish followers of Yeshua also attended. It was in this congregation that Isaac met his wife-to-be, Rachael. They had both participated in a mission trip to Africa with a relief organization who provides nutrient

33

dense food products to malnourished children. Both Isaac's and Rachael's hearts were deeply touched by incredible need in the lives of the malnourished children they met. They were shocked to learn that close to ten million children per year die, due to malnutrition.

Upon his return from Africa, Isaac decided to increase the percentage of his monthly cash flow allocated to his 'Offering' jar in order to help more of the malnourished children. He was able to make this readjustment by moving a little more money from his Spending jar to his Offering jar.

Shortly after Isaac and Rachael married, Isaac was questioning what his unique purpose and calling really was. His heart had been so touched by the Lord to help alleviate the problem of malnutrition in developing countries that he and Rachael had been talking about selling his businesses, going to Bible school and giving the rest of their lives as missionaries in Africa. With these kinds of questions in his heart, Isaac asked to spend a little time with his father to get his counsel about their future.

As Rachael and Isaac, sat down on the big sofa in his parent's living room, Papa opened the conversation by saying, "Isaac, what do you think a calling is, and who has one?"

Pondering the question for a few moments, Isaac responded by saying, "I have usually heard that word, 'calling' applied to people in full time ministry, like a Rabbi, Pastor, or Missionary. I guess a calling is a unique and special guidance that someone receives from God to serve Him in full time ministry."

Papa then responded, "Son, only three percent of all people serve God as Rabbis, Pastors, Missionaries or people who earn their living from preaching or serving in a congregation. Do you think that God has just left the 97% on their own to pursue their own affairs?"

"Well, no," replied Isaac. "But the 97% of all other people are involved in secular work. I'm not sure if they have a calling."

"Interesting that you should bring up secular work. Isaac, do you know the actual dictionary definition of the word 'secular?'" queried Papa.

"No, I've never looked it up," responded Isaac.

"As I recall, the word 'secular' actually means, something like having nothing to do with God, or 'temporal, not relating to eternity[1].' So what type of work would a person, who has given his whole life to God, do that 'has nothing to do with God,' or is 'temporal and not related to eternity?' Isaac, have you given the rest of your life to God? Does He have your permission to do anything He wants with the rest of your life?"

"Yes, Papa," replied Isaac. "When we were there together in Israel, and I realized that Jesus gave up His whole life for me, I gave the rest of my life to Him. I told God that evening that from then on, I would be like a dollar bill in His pocket. He could spend me on whatever He wants. So I guess for me, any work that I do would be because I believe that God wants me to do that particular work. So, I guess if God wanted me to be a businessman that would be my calling from God, just as much as if He wanted me to be a missionary in Uganda helping malnourished children."

"Now you're catching my point, Isaac," said his father. "**Every one of us has a calling from God, not just special people.** If one hundred percent of all the people gave their lives to God the way you just described, and gave Him permission to direct their lives, would we then have 100% of the people working as Pastors, Evangelists, and Missionaries? Of course not! God calls people to own businesses, be airline pilots, engineers, truck drivers, actors, movie directors, senators, mayors, school

---

[1] http://www.merriam-webster.com/dictionary/secular

teachers, television news anchors, as well as to be pastors, and missionaries.

Papa continued, "Many people think that in order to truly serve God, they must be paid as a pastor, missionary, or religious worker of some sort. Of course this is not true. Each of us is called to use our gifts and skills to be a productive contributor to society and to glorify and worship God in all we do. If you have found what God has called you to do, and you are doing so with all your heart, seeking God's direction every day, then your work becomes worship to God."

"Isaac, I have recently read a wonderful book by a godly businessman, Os Hillman, that talks about how each one of us is called to be a change agent in the sphere of society in which we function. God needs people to manifest His glory and be change agents in every sphere of society. So it doesn't matter if you are called to function in business, politics, science and technology, media, or as a foreign missionary. You are still called to be a change agent to influence people for God's Kingdom in any of those realms in which you may be called to work."

> If you have found what God has called you to do, and you are doing so with all your heart, seeking God's direction every day, then your work becomes worship to God."

Holding up the book for Isaac and Rachael to see, Papa continued, "I'd like to give you a copy of this book and have both you and Rachael read it. It is called **Change Agent** by Os Hillman[2]. I really love the subtitle, '*Engaging Your Passion To Be The One Who Makes a Difference.*' Isaac, that's what I want for your life: to engage your passion to make a difference."

---

[2] Hillman, Os, *Change Agent* (Lake Mary, FL: Charisma House: 2011)

"Great, Papa, I'd love to read that book. But how do I know exactly what God wants me to do, and what my calling really is?" inquired Isaac.

"My experience has been that God usually places within a person desires and abilities that facilitate the purpose and calling from God for that person's life. So, my question to you would be the following. What do you lie awake at night thinking and dreaming about? What do you love to do? What are you really good at? And if you could do anything you like, what would it be?" asked Papa.

"Well, I love business," replied Isaac. "I lie awake dreaming about how to increase the volume of my current business, new ways I can serve my customers, and a new business I might start. However, my heart was also really touched in Africa by being able to make a difference in the lives of the malnourished children. Because I want to serve God with all my heart, that's why Rachael and I were thinking of going to Bible school and then giving our lives to be missionaries in Africa."

"Isaac," Papa started. "While I understand how your heart was touched by the kids in Africa, I don't think that this is your primary calling. Many people have the skill set to serve malnourished kids in Africa, but very few people have the anointing, gifting, and wisdom you have to start and run businesses and generate cash flow. You can certainly use much of the money, with which God blesses you in business, as a tool to help provide nutrition to malnourished children. However, I believe that you would be missing the call of God on your life if you sold your businesses and spent your life ministering to children in Africa. You can go on short-term trips to help the orphans personally, but I don't believe that this is your primary calling."

"I think you're probably right, Papa," replied Isaac. "But, I have another question that comes to mind. Sometimes I have thought that if I pursue business instead of becoming a missionary, that I am pursuing money instead of pursuing my calling and vision. I now am beginning to see that business is my calling, but how do money and vision relate?"

"That's an excellent question, Isaac," replied Papa. "The 96% thinkers will always pursue money instead of pursuing vision. I have found that just the opposite is true. If you pursue your God-given vision, money naturally follows vision. While lack of knowledge and lack of vision are the greatest hindrances to success, the 96% thinkers always think that the greatest hindrance to their success is lack of money. From listening to many Christians who think this way, you would think that there must be a Bible verse that says, '*Where there is no money, My people perish,*' or '*My people are destroyed for lack of money.*' Of course there is no scripture verse like that. However, the Bible does say that people perish for **lack of vision** and that people are destroyed for **lack of knowledge.**

Proverbs 29:18

18 Where there is no vision, the people perish: but he that keepeth the law, happy is he.

Hosea 4:6

6 My people are destroyed for lack of knowledge.

"You're for sure right about that, Papa," said Isaac. Most people around me complain about needing more money as if more money were the answer to all their problems."

"Very true," said Papa. "In reality, most people have not even thought through the reasons why they might need money. Money has no inherent value. It is only a tool that can be used to accomplish a vision. Probably, the very first reason someone would need money would be for 'provision.' Let's talk about the relationship of provision to vision for a few minutes. It is very important to understand this relationship."

"Of course, all of us need food, clothing, shelter, transportation, etcetera," continued Papa. "However, a focus on obtaining provision usually results in a lack thereof. As I said before, provision naturally follows vision. The word *provision* is made up of two parts: the prefix *pro* and the root word *vision*. What are the meanings of these two parts of the word? *Pro* means, 'for,' or 'in favor of;'" Vision signifies 'the ability to see the end goal or destination when you are still at the beginning.' Webster's dictionary defines vision as: 'the ability to perceive something not actually visible, as through mental acuteness or keen foresight.[3] So provision is that which comes to you at the beginning for the purpose of taking you to the end goal or destination. Provision then is that which comes for the vision."

"So vision must precede provision. If there is no vision, there is no need for 'that which comes for the vision,' or provision. Where there is no vision, people perish, because provision only comes to support vision. No vision – no provision. So the means to obtain provision is to pursue and clarify vision."

"Is that why you were talking to us about clearly discerning our calling and vision?" asked Rachael.

"Exactly," replied Papa. "While most of the 96% do not have, and cannot express a clear calling or vision for their lives, the 4% can clearly and succinctly articulate their calling and vision. The 96% prepare their children to have an 'occupation' and earn a 'living.' An occupation is simply something that occupies your time until you die, and the purpose of 'a living,' is simply to live. But life is more than just living and occupying your time. Life is about purpose! The 4% prepare their children to fulfill a calling and destiny. As we already talked about, a calling is what God has called you to and is the purpose for which God put you on the earth.

"The 96% work for money fulfilling someone else's vision, while the 4% work for vision and make money work for them. For the 96%, money is their master and they do what they do for

---

[3] http://www.merriam-webster.com/dictionary/vision

money. Since money is their master, God becomes the servant to get the 96% more money. For the 4%, money is their servant, and they do what they do to fulfill a calling given to them by God. Since God is the master, money becomes their servant, to fulfill God's purpose and calling on their lives."

Papa continued, "It is simple to tell whether someone really has thought through and can articulate the vision and calling for their life or not. I travel a fair amount in my business. Many times I have initiated conversation with people sitting next to me on airplanes. Sometimes I have had a conversation with seatmates very similar to the following:

"What do you do for a living?"

"I work for such and such company, or sell this product, or work at this factory."

"Do you like that kind of work?"

"Not really."

"How many hours a week do you work and for how many years have you been doing this work?"

"Oh, about 45 to 50 hours a week and I've been doing this for about 25 years."

"So you have been doing something that you really don't like 50 hours a week for 25 years. Why are you continuing to do that work?"

"For the money. I have to work."

"Why do you need the money?"

"At this point," continued Papa, "my seatmates usually look a little puzzled by the question, as if to say, 'Well duh, what a stupid question.' But they are usually polite and say, 'I need money to pay my bills; you know, for my house, my car, my food, my clothes.'"

"Why do you need a house, food, car and clothes?"

"Now they look a little miffed and say, "Obviously, without a house, clothes, and food, I will die."

"Then sometimes I ask one final question to get to the bottom and find vision. 'So why do you need to live?'"

"At this question," continued Papa, "most people just look at me with a blank stare. This question is requesting an articulation of the purpose for which God has placed that person on the planet. At least 96% of the people have never thought that through, and cannot give me a clear articulate purpose for their existence and vision for their life. If they can't answer the question, I then usually relieve the tension by telling them that most people have not thought this through and also cannot give a clear answer to this question. I then usually let them know that God placed them on the planet with a unique purpose and destiny and that He loves them very much and would love to reveal to them the purpose for which He created them."

"Wow! That's amazing," said Isaac. "I guess I never thought about it that way. I'm not sure if I would have had a clear answer either before today. Now, I'm going to pray about it, and get a clear answer I can articulate."

"You know, Isaac," continued Papa. "In order to accomplish any purpose, you can either use vision or use money. If you have a specific vision to accomplish a purpose, and you are able to clearly articulate that vision, many other people will invest their money in your vision. However, if you have no vision, or you can't clearly articulate your vision, no one will invest in you. In that case, you will have to simply write a check to accomplish the goal. If you don't have vision or money, regarding that goal you will perish, as Proverbs 29:18 declares."

> In order to accomplish any purpose, you can either use vision or use money.

"Many years ago," Papa said, "I heard an acquaintance describe this principle. This man had become very prosperous in his particular business, and when asked what the key to his success was, he stated, 'It's television. That's the key to my success.'"

"'What do you mean?' inquired a listener. 'Did you build your business by doing infomercials, or television advertisements, or what?'"

41

"'No, no!' replied the successful businessman. 'I'm not referring to the electronic income reducer that sits in your family room and entertains people. I built my business through telling the vision. **Tell a Vision, not television.** I have a very powerful product and an intensely compelling reason why people need my product. So in the beginning, I shared the vision of my business plan with some potential investors, who became intrigued with my product and plan and invested the money I needed to begin the business. I continued to tell the vision to my sales representatives and consumers and built a powerful base of product consumers and sales representatives, who have continued to cause my business to grow and prosper. So the key to my success has been to tell others my vision.'"

Papa, turned toward Isaac and Rachael and said, "You know, Isaac, lack of money is never the hindrance to accomplishment. It is either lack of vision or lack of knowledge. But it seems that most people believe that lack of money is the primary obstacle."

"You're right Papa," exclaimed Isaac. What you shared just reminded me of the experience of one of the ladies who was on the recent missions trip with us in Africa. Each of us had to raise our own money to finance our airfare and expenses on the trip. A retired schoolteacher, Elsie, who was on the trip with us, shared how she learned this exact principle of Tell A Vision."

"Yeah, that's right," Rachael chimed in. "She told us that just six weeks before we were to leave on the trip, she desperately wanted to go and felt called by God to go, but had no money. She let the leader of the charitable organization we went with know of her desire, but lack of financial resource. She was focused on the provision and didn't understand the principle of sharing the vision. She believed that for lack of money, her ability to go on the trip would perish, or not be fulfilled."

Continuing, Rachael said, "The group leader, apparently realizing the problem, then suggested that Elsie use 'tell a vision.' He suggested she write a letter outlining her vision to participate on this team, to help the malnourished children in Uganda, and send it to her personal friends, and several of the churches in which she had conducted life-changing seminars here in the U.S. in the past."

Isaac jumped in, "Elsie then sent the letter, and later shared with us that she was shocked at the financial response. Within about two weeks other people who believed in her ministry, had sent her more than enough money to participate in the mission trip to Africa. Since that time, apparently, Elsie has now gone on several other mission trips, continuing to give her life to support malnourished children. She is now planning to move to Africa and is in the process of raising enough money to support herself full time in this humanitarian work."

"Great example, you two!" exclaimed Papa. "You are quick learners. So in review, people do not perish for lack of money, but only for lack of knowledge or lack of vision. It is also interesting to note that the 96% thinkers who suddenly find themselves with large amounts of money are very rarely able to retain the money they have received. We have heard many stories about those, who have won multi-million dollar lottery jackpots, only to find themselves destitute and without financial resource in just a few short years. Why is this?"

Before they could answer, Papa answered his own question, "I believe this is so because most of the 96% thinkers lack the wisdom and vision to administrate larger sums of money. On the other hand, we have also heard stories of wealthy 4% thinkers who have been stripped of large fortunes only to regain their wealth again in a few short years. Why? I believe that this is probably because the vision within the 4% thinker generates wealth again in a very short period of time. So, in the long term, a person with strong, clear vision (4% thinker) and no money will be much better off financially than a person with lots of money and no strong, clear vision" (96% thinker) *(Matthew 19:26)*.

"That seems so simple," said Isaac. "Why do you think it is, Papa, that in our day, so many people focus on money or provision? Has it always been that way?"

"No son," said Papa. "In past times, even the general population focused more on vision than on money or provision. However, over the past fifty or sixty years, values here in our modern society have really changed. In past times, here in the United States, even the vast majority of the ninety-six percent valued purpose, destiny, and calling above money. At that time, the concept that I have been placed here by God, to fulfill a destiny and purpose much greater than myself, and that this purpose will require self sacrifice for the benefit of others was commonly embraced. While today this type of lifestyle is reserved for only the very few 'special' people like Mother Theresa, in past times, this lifestyle of individual sacrifice and living for a purpose much greater than self was common to many people in society."

"For many today, character has been replaced by convenience. The former value of <u>self-sacrifice</u> has largely been exchanged for the value of <u>self-gratification.</u> Lack of a strong sense of purpose and destiny produces a self-focus and certain feeling of emptiness and lack of fulfillment in life. Many people today live for diversion and entertainment to fill up an empty, meaningless life. Self-focused people then see money as a primary means to gratify and entertain self, to help comfort and ease the emotional pain of the futility and purposelessness of life. People living for a purpose beyond self see money as simply a tool, to accomplish a vision in fulfillment of a divine destiny or calling."

Papa continued, "So what would be the purpose of a college education?"

Again, answering his own question, "In past times, when the value of self sacrifice was still held, the purpose of higher education was to gain the knowledge and skills to make a difference in the world and to fulfill one's calling and destiny. In modern times, in which the value of self-gratification is held, the purpose of higher education is to prepare oneself to make more money to spend to be able to have bigger and better things and live a more lavish lifestyle."

"Here, let me read you a quote from a book on marriage written by a friend of mine, Craig Hill, entitled, *Help! My Spouse Wants Out.*[4] In this section I want you to hear, the values of a 20-year old young man in 1942. Contrast these values from the last century with those values held by most 20-year old young people in our current time. The contrast is quite shocking. Let me read you a section."

Papa picked up the book, opened to a well-worn section, and read:

One of the prime results of this value exchange is that children growing up in this environment have lost the sense of intrinsic worth and destiny. In times past, each person growing up felt unique, and special. He felt valuable to God and to society; as though he were here for a purpose far greater than himself and that he had something unique to contribute to society and to the kingdom of God. It was not that long ago that young people used to experience a sense of destiny and reason to live far beyond themselves. I recently read a letter, which my father wrote to his father in 1942, explaining his future plans after the war. My father grew up in a traditional denominational church and thus did not have at this point in his life a strong sense of being led by the Lord. However, it is interesting to note the values he held as a 20-year old man in 1942. I would like to quote a portion of this letter below.

---

[4] Hill, Craig, *Help? My Spouse Wants Out* (Littleton, CO, Family Foundations International, 1996)

Dear Dad,

As an outgrowth of our short talk on occupational interests this afternoon, I would like to indicate my plans for the future to avoid misunderstandings....

After the war I plan to return to school to study many different scientific, military, and political fields. My main interests lie in the many fields of science such as medicine, genetics, physics, chemistry, astronomy; and certain scientific, psychological, mental effects connected with medicine. The only reason that I would go into politics or military affairs is if they are as corrupt as they have been so many times in the past. That is, if we win the war and lose the peace so as to find ourselves in just as bad a position as if Germany had won the war, then it would seem necessary to go into a political war against these darn political ring leaders that frequently run our congress. In my case I don't give a darn about money. As long as I can get enough to eat and a little clothes to wear, **I will spend the rest of the time wherever it can do the most good,** *whether its fighting international military wars, or fighting political ring leaders, or trying to lick some baffling scientific problems.....*

After the war I plan to go back to school for the rest of my life to study and try to solve as many of these problems as possible. This work of course pays very little, so financially I plan to be practically dead broke all of my life. If a person works with a University you will perhaps receive 4 or 5 thousand dollars per year after considerable number of years of experience, but at the same time you are perhaps buying 3 or 4 thousand dollars worth of equipment for your research that your department couldn't afford to buy for you. This perhaps leaves you with less than $1000 per year. All in all, you can only expect to barely make a living & never save up any money. That's just the type of work I like in that I detest high salary men that keep spending their money on themselves or feathering their own nests. This is a field that you can

really be a service to your country-men to develop methods &
apparatus for relieving pain and curing the diseased."
(Gilman Hill, July 26, 1942)

"The thing that was shocking to me was the sense of
destiny and purpose beyond himself that my father
possessed as a twenty-year old. He definitely held the
value of self-sacrifice far above self-gratification. His
purpose was to be of service to his countrymen, have
enough food and clothing to live and then spend the
rest of his time wherever it could do the most good.
After reading this letter, I asked my father if this was
an unusual attitude, which he uniquely possessed. He
told me that this was not unique at all. Most of his
friends and those, with whom he was in school, all had
a similar attitude. Apparently at that time, there was a
value held by many people of self-sacrificial living for
the good of society and others. This value has all but
departed as a lifestyle from our present society. This is
something, which I believe that God wants to restore
to His Church."

"As you consider how you will relate to your spouse
and your present circumstance, this fundamental value
must be examined. For whom are you living? Are you
living for Jesus Christ, His name, His kingdom, His
will and for the benefit and welfare of your children
and others who don't know Him; or are you living for
yourself, your short-term happiness and emotional
well-being? Do you embrace the basic value of self-
sacrificial living or the value of selfish living? These
questions are critical for you to answer in your own
heart before God."

For a Christian, happiness is not really the goal of
life. In the Kingdom of God the goal is obedience to
Jesus and the expansion and promotion of His

47

Kingdom. Joy and fulfillment of life are not the goals, but rather are the by products that come from serving Jesus. One who seeks the byproduct rather than the goal usually misses out on both. Jesus said that seeking your own pleasure and happiness would cause you to lose the very thing you are seeking.

Mark 8:34-35

"If anyone wishes to come after Me, let him deny himself, and take up his cross, and follow Me. For whoever wishes to save his own life shall lose it; but whoever loses his life for My sake and the gospel's shall save it".

So serving Jesus and serving self are opposite goals and are incompatible with each other. Serving Jesus is based on the value of self-sacrifice, and serving self is based on the value of self-gratification. God has never forced anyone to serve Him. It is a free choice for each of us. However, we must recognize that there is a choice, and again our strategies must be based on the actual values we really do hold.[5]

Putting the book down, Papa said, "So it appears that people have not always focused on money and provision. In past times, many people were men and women of character, who focused on vision and calling. This is the critical point, Isaac. Pray, talk together, and establish a clear, focused vision. Then pursue your vision with all your heart, and God will always see to it that you have plenty of provision. But on the other hand, don't avoid money, or business, thinking that you are being spiritual or

---

[5] *ibid.* pp. 51-53

pleasing God. I believe that business is your primary calling," concluded Papa.

"Yes, I think you're right," replied Isaac. "Thanks Papa for helping us think this through. Rachael and I will pray together about this and clarify our calling and vision."

Over the next few days as Isaac and Rachael talked and prayed about this, it became clear that Isaac was indeed called to business and philanthropy. His passion really was business, and he was called by God to be a change agent in that sphere of influence in society. That is where his mind naturally went when left to himself. In addition, thinking about the number of malnourished children whose mortality rate and quality of life could be significantly changed for the better through money provided from his 'Offerings' jar fueled Isaac all the more to build his business and operate it more efficiently.

This discussion with Papa, along with his subsequent prayer times and conversation with Rachael, had really clarified the vision for Isaac's life. He now knew that he was called by God to start and operate businesses, and to use money as a tool to provide jobs for others, and to support malnourished children in Africa. This gave him a very clear reason in his heart for why he was doing what he was doing. So Isaac continued to grow his financing company and to manage his car wash and real estate investments. The money from their 'Offerings' jar, that Isaac and Rachael were able to contribute to help the children in Africa, soon increased to over ten thousand dollars per month.

Meanwhile, Isaac kept in touch with his former schoolmate Billy, now called Bill of course. Bill unfortunately had no wise counsel from his father. After high school, Bill went on to college and got a degree in engineering. Bill chose this area of study not because of calling, but due to of the hope of making a lot of money. After college, Bill married Sue and got a great job with an engineering firm making over $80,000 per year to start. Bill and Sue purchased a beautiful new $300,000 house and got a great loan from the bank with 0% down payment, and an interest-only monthly payment for five years.

Bill had never thought through his vision, and consequently purchased a new house, new cars, many appliances, and belonged to a country club at which he loved to play golf. In addition, because Bill had only one jar for his money, he and Sue created a lifestyle that consumed 100% of their monthly cash flow to service the monthly obligations for their house mortgage payment, car payments, credit card payments and country club dues. Bill and Sue became focused on money, and a couple times in the early years of their marriage lost money on "get rich quick schemes" to which their friends introduced them. Sue got a job, not because she wanted to work or was called to work, but rather because they needed the money to help pay their bills.

Bill and Sue were really touched by a charitable organization they heard about at their church that was helping to free child sex slaves in Thailand and Cambodia. There were teams on the ground in these countries going into the brothels and actually taking these young girls out of forced prostitution. The organization was then providing homes and helping these young girls finish their education and to come into vital relationship with God. Bill and Sue really wanted to be able to go themselves to see this work in Southeast Asia and to give substantial amounts of money to it. However, Bill and Sue were never able to do so, because all the money they had each month was completely consumed by the monthly payments to which they had already committed themselves.

Bill and Sue frequently lamented the fact that they didn't have enough money to do what was really in their hearts to help these young girls. Isaac and Rachael attempted to share with them the principle of provision following vision. Once, Isaac even asked Bill, where was the scripture that said, "for lack of money my people perish." However, Bill never did capture the concept, and thus never did change his focus off of money to pursue the vision and calling God had for his life.

Secret Number 2: Focus on vision not on provision. Discover your purpose and calling from God. Choose your career or profession according to calling not according to money. Then pursue your calling and vision with all your heart and expect provision to naturally follow vision.

Reflection

1. Explain what it would look like in your life to focus on vision rather than on provision.

2. Describe your relationship with God.

   a. Have you dedicated your life to Jesus Christ, and given Him permission to direct the rest of your life?

3. Have you realized before that you have a calling and destiny from God?

4. Describe the clearest statement of your vision for your life, as you understand it at this point. (If your vision is not yet clear, you might ask others to pray for you to get a clear vision.)

5. Describe how you could engage your passion to make a difference in the world.

6. Describe how your vision pushes you out to live a life beyond yourself that glorifies God and benefits others.

7. In what ways have you believed in your own life the adage, "For lack of <u>money,</u> My people perish?"

8. In what way can you utilize the concept of Tell A Vision to move the vision forward in your life?

CHAPTER 3

INVEST IN MULTIPLICATION

Third Secret: Part 1 –
Invest in Things That Multiply

The third secret that the 4% understand and practice has to do with how they utilize their money. While the 96% tend to use most, or all of their money to purchase things that depreciate, the 4% allocate a significant portion of their money to invest in things that MULTIPLY. As a result, the 4% thinkers never borrow for personal consumption or purchase depreciating items on credit. Because they put their money in only one jar, frequently, the 96% thinkers spend all the money they have and then purchase additional items on credit, or borrow money in order to fund obligations, necessities or contingencies for which they hadn't planned.

Isaac continued through his early twenty's to build his finance company and to increase his real estate holdings. One evening, while he and Rachael were having dinner with his parents, Isaac asked his father why there seemed to be such a difference in his lifestyle and experience than that of many of his friends, specifically Bill, Bob and Jim, with whom he had gone to school.

"Papa," started Isaac. "I've been wondering why most of my friends don't seem to make very wise financial decisions. Many choices that seem obvious to me don't seem to be obvious to my friends like, Bill, Bob and Jim. For example, all three of these families have run up significant credit card balances and continue to talk about financing improvements on their homes and purchasing newer cars on credit."

"I saw something very ironic just last weekend at a meeting held at our congregation. Bill, who loves God with all his heart as I do, wore a tee shirt to the meeting with the words written, **'ONE MASTER.'** Of course, the Master, to which he was referring, was Jesus, the Messiah. However, I was remembering the teaching you gave me when I was ten years old, when you showed me the Bible verse from Proverbs 22:7. You asked me the question whether I wanted to grow up to be rich or poor, a slave or a master. You taught me that this verse tells us that the borrower is a servant to the master. I thought it was so ironic that Bill would wear this tee shirt declaring that he has one Master, when I know for a fact that he has borrowed a lot of money from various credit cards and finance companies, and thus in reality is a servant to many masters. One of his masters is so bold that they even put their name on their card. They call it 'Master Card,' to make sure you know who they are."

"You know, Papa," continued Isaac. "I think, if the truth were known, very few people in our church would only have one master, and could wear that tee shirt with integrity. You know what else, Papa? I think most of my friends have allocated 100% of their monthly cash flow to simply meet their basic life necessities and pay their monthly debt obligations. If God personally appeared in physical form in our church and asked us as a congregation to participate financially in a missions project, most people couldn't do so, whether they wanted to or not. One hundred percent of their monthly cash flow is already allocated to their debt obligations. So in reality they can't obey The Master because they have many other 'masters' who must be satisfied first. At least, I know this is the case with Bill and Sue and most of my other friends."

"I'm proud of you, Isaac," exclaimed his father. "You have learned much already at a young age. You have just described another difference between the thinking of the 4% and that of the 96%. The 96% invest their money in things that depreciate, while the 4% invest their money in things that multiply. The very first commandment that God gave man in the Garden of Eden was *'to be fruitful and multiply'* (Genesis 1:28). So God expects us to not only be fruitful, but also to multiply.

> The 96% invest their money in things that depreciate, while the 4% invest their money in things that multiply.

Regarding lending and borrowing, lending causes money to multiply though the collection of compound interest, while borrowing causes money to dissipate through the loss of compound interest. Wisdom tells us that, when we abide by God's principles, we will be blessed. The scripture tells us in

Deuteronomy 28:12-13

"...and you shall lend to many nations, but you shall not borrow. 13 The LORD will make you the head and not the tail, and you only will be above, and you will not be underneath, if you listen to the commandments of the LORD your God, which I charge you today, to observe them carefully."

"Lending," continued Papa, "multiplies the value of your money. Borrowing depletes the value of your money. While borrowing is not categorically wrong, Isaac, the cost of borrowing, namely the interest, must always be significantly less than the value created through the investment. It may be wise to borrow to capitalize a business or to invest in a property or asset that multiplies in value, at a much greater rate than the cost of the interest charged to borrow the money. However, the 96% frequently are willing to pay interest through borrowing to invest in something that not only doesn't increase in value at all, but actually depreciates in value over the course of their loan. It sounds like this is what several of your friends have done."

"That's exactly true, Papa," exclaimed Isaac. "Several of my friends have actually borrowed money to finance a car or even go on a vacation. These are certainly not things that increase in value, and instead only serve to make them slaves to lenders."

"Very true, Isaac," exclaimed his father. "You were talking about your friend with the 'One Master' tee shirt. I believe you could actually wear this shirt, because you have no personal debt, and a substantial personal monthly positive cash flow."

"Yes, but I have borrowed money and have debt payments on my apartment complexes and car wash businesses. I've already paid off all of my rental houses. But I am a slave to lenders who hold the notes on my real estate investments, so I'm not sure I could wear the tee shirt either." said Isaac

Papa responded, "I think you can. You control 100% of your personal monthly cash flow, because you have no personal debt. This qualifies you to wear the tee shirt. While you have borrowed money to finance your car wash businesses and your apartment buildings, the monthly cash flow from these projects far exceed the interest payments, and the equity value of these businesses and properties continues to grow, and far exceeds the loan balance on each of them. You could view the loans on these investments really as a conditional sale. At any moment, you would be willing to let the bank have these properties for the loan balance. Of course, there is a danger of the value of these properties declining in the future, but in this season, the asset values far exceeds the loan balances. So, I believe that in this season, it has been wise to borrow for these investments, as the increase in equity value and monthly cash flow has far exceeded the interest cost of the borrowed money."

Continuing, Papa said, "Isaac, you were mentioning that people in your congregation could not respond to God financially, even if He physically appeared and asked for their participation because most of them have already committed one hundred percent of their monthly cash flow to other masters (creditors). The consequence of this is that congregational leaders are not then able to raise the necessary money from the people to build buildings. The congregational leadership then frequently does the same thing that the 96% thinkers have done. They go to the bank and borrow money in order to build a building.

Now, if God wants to prune the congregation, or the pastor must preach something unpopular, some people will leave the congregation. This could put pressure on the pastor and leaders who now are responsible to meet the monthly payment on the building. Even if the pastor and leaders have pure hearts after God, there is still an undue pressure placed upon them because they have allowed themselves to become slaves to a lender. Under such pressure, the pastor may decide not to preach the unpopular message in order to preserve the money needed to pay the mortgage. Now Isaac, who controls what is preached in that congregation?"

"I suppose it is fear, generated by the spirit of Mammon,[1] that now dictates what is preached, making the pastor and congregational leaders slaves to a bank," replied Isaac.

"Exactly!' exclaimed Papa. "I don't think that this is God's plan, or pattern."

---

[1] For more understanding on the spirit of Mammon see the book, *Wealth, Riches and Money*, by Craig Hill, (Littleton, CO, Family Foundations International, 2001), Chapter 1

"I was just thinking of the pattern we have in the Bible for funding facilities or buildings in which to meet. After the exodus of our people from Egypt, there came a time to build a tabernacle in which to worship God. Moses and the leaders asked the congregation of people to bring offerings in order to construct the tabernacle." Papa opened the Bible application on his iphone and read:

Exodus 36:5-7

"5 and they said to Moses, "The people are bringing much more than enough for the construction work which the LORD commanded us to perform." 6 So Moses issued a command, and a proclamation was circulated throughout the camp, saying, "Let no man or woman any longer perform work for the contributions of the sanctuary." Thus the people were restrained from bringing any more. 7 For the material they had was sufficient and more than enough for all the work, to perform it."

"Isaac, when have you ever heard the pastor in your congregation tell people to stop giving because they have already brought more than enough?" asked Isaac's father.

"Never, Papa," chuckled Isaac.

"Well, that is exactly what happened in ancient Israel. I was wondering how they were able to do so in that day, and we are not able to come even close in our day. I was asking myself, 'What was the difference then? Were the people more generous? Or they had more resource?' Then it dawned on me the difference was the people in that time had no debt, and thus were in control of 100% of their own resources. They only had one Master, God. Today most people are in great debt and thus have given control of their resources to many other masters (creditors). Most people are not able to be directed by God in their finances, even if they want to, because they have already delegated authority over their resources, and become slaves to their multiple other masters. This is the primary reason this biblical pattern of funding buildings, in which to congregate, does not work today."

"Papa," queried Isaac, "how did our society get in such a mess? I think that more than 90% of the people here in North America carry personal debt. Almost everyone has a mortgage on his home. Has it always been that way?"

"No, son, it hasn't," replied Isaac's father. "Four generations ago, maybe even three generations ago, almost no one had any debt. At that time, it would not have even entered into the mind of a young couple, who wanted a house to go to a bank and borrow money for thirty years in order to own a house. Today, that thought would come into the mind of probably about 96% of the young people. In fact, many people would think that it is not possible to own a house without a mortgage. However, I don't have a mortgage now and never have borrowed money from a bank for my house. You have never borrowed money from a bank for your house. One hundred years ago, no one borrowed from a bank to own a house."

"How were people able to own a house then?" asked Isaac.

"In those days, a concept that we have always practiced in our community, and still do today, was commonly practiced by everyone. This was the practice of generational blessing. Parents and grandparents felt a responsibility to help their children and grandchildren who were just starting out in life. Typically four generations ago, when a young couple was ready to have their own home, the parents and grandparents provided the finances for whatever materials were needed. Many times natural materials, such as lumber were used and provided by parents. Then the entire extended family came together to provide the labor necessary to build the new house. In this way, each generation fulfilled the ancient proverb that states: *'a good man leaves an inheritance to his children's children' (Proverbs 13:22b).*

"Today, somehow most families have lost the concept of generational blessing," continued Papa.

"So, one hundred years ago, the thought would not have occurred to anyone to go to a bank and take out a thirty-year mortgage to purchase a house," said Isaac. "But today that thought would occur to at least 96% of all Americans. What changed in that time span?"

"Well," started Papa, "I don't know, Isaac, if you believe in a literal Satan and demonic spirits, but I have come to believe that they are real. I have found that there are real spiritual battles that take place in our society and that Satan implements strategic plans to enslave people to himself."

"I believe that too, Papa," quickly added Isaac.

"Well then, I don't know if it happened exactly this way, or not. But I believe that about 100 years ago there was a global strategy conference in hell. Satan gathered all the demons and announced that he was looking for a new strategy by which he could enslave nations and generations to himself. The spirit of Mammon (Matthew 6:24) raised his hand and stated that he had a plan.

> About 100 years ago there was a global strategy conference in hell.

"Mammon began, 'I think that we can use a principle I learned from the Bible. Proverbs 22:7 tells us that the borrower is slave to the lender. We already have many institutions and individuals that we control from hell. They are completely dedicated to serve me, and I control them through their love of money. So we will begin to use these institutions and people to make money available to borrow at interest. Others who then borrow the money become slaves of the lenders, whom we control.'"

Papa continued his discourse, "Satan then asked, 'But how do we force people to borrow?'

"'No, we don't force them at all,' smirked Mammon. People will voluntarily borrow the money.'"

"'What?' railed Satan. 'You think that people will voluntarily agree to be slaves to institutions and people we already control from hell? They won't do that.'"

"'Maybe not many, at first,' said Mammon. 'But we will continue to deceive people and get them accustomed to the idea. So at first we will have only a few who will borrow. But after a few short decades, I think we will have most of the entire society acclimated to the idea of debt and most people will borrow and become our slaves.'"

"Very clever," interjected Isaac.

"Indeed," continued Papa. "Satan then said, 'But I really wanted a strategy that would affect the Christians too. I don't think this will work with them.'"

"'Sure it will,' said Mammon. 'They will do the same as everyone else.'"

"'You mean to tell me that you think that people in relationship with God, filled with the Holy Spirit, will just voluntarily bow down and become slaves of institutions and individuals that we control from hell? They'll never do that. They're not that stupid!'"

"Again Mammon countered, 'Maybe not many at first, but after some time, more and more will, as we deceive them too, and introduce this idea to them as normal. I believe that eventually we will even get their pastors and leaders to borrow for their church buildings and thus subject their institutions to be our slaves. We will make the concept of debt seem so completely normal, such that after several decades, families, companies, churches, cities and even nations will become our slaves through debt. Let's just introduce the concept and see what happens over a little time.'"

"Satan mused for a few moments, and barked, 'Okay Mammon, go ahead with your plan. We will see if our deception is really as strong as you think, and people will voluntarily submit themselves to be our slaves through debt. It is hard to believe that people could be so foolish and short sighted, but perhaps you are right. Soon we will see!'"

Papa then concluded, "And the rest, Isaac, is history. That is how I think we got from where we were one hundred years ago, when no one borrowed from banks and finance companies, to where we are now, when most people take on large amounts of personal debt. I think this is the deception of an entire culture and society."

"Wow, Papa. That's incredible," exclaimed Isaac. "So if I understand correctly, the 4% lend and don't borrow on non-multiplying assets because they are focused on investing their money in things that multiply, and lending money causes the money to multiply, while borrowing depletes it. The 96% don't understand or think about multiplication, and don't have any jars, so they simply spend all their money from their one jar and then borrow more to meet their needs and wants. Is that correct?"

"Yes son, you got it."

Isaac then asked, "But what about God's supernatural multiplication? How does that factor into the equation? For example, the time when Jesus multiplied the food from one personal lunch to feed several thousand people comes to mind. Do you think that we should still expect God to do things like that today?"

Isaac's father grinned, "Absolutely son! If Satan and demonic spirits are supernaturally deceiving people, how much more is God supernaturally acting to benefit the lives of His people? But again, there is something I have noticed about the way that the 4% think that attracts God's supernatural multiplication."

"How do they think?" quickly asked Isaac.

"Well," started Papa, "While the 96% tend to focus on what they don't have, the 4% tend to focus on what they do have. The 4% many times expect God's supernatural multiplication of a very small initial amount. So, for example, in the story you mentioned, Jesus' disciples were baffled as to how they might feed several thousand people (John 6:4-14). Unfortunately, they were focused on that which they did not have. Jesus had asked his disciples to feed the people. They immediately began to tell Jesus that they didn't have enough food. They didn't have enough money. And even if they did, there was no town nearby in which they might buy food. "

"Finally, one follower, Andrew, changed the focus from what they didn't have to what they did have. My paraphrase of what he said is: 'One little boy here has his own personal lunch of five bread rolls and two fish that he is willing to donate. I don't know what good that will do among so many, but that is what we have.' Jesus then took that personal lunch and released God's supernatural multiplication such that five thousand men and their families were fed from that one personal lunch."

"Isaac, the point is this," continued Papa. "God can naturally or supernaturally multiply by huge factors, such as 100, 1000, or even 10,000. However, even ten thousand times zero is still zero $(10,000 \times 0 = 0)$. A person who continues to focus on and present to God what he does not have, or in other words zero, will never experience God's multiplication. Even one times ten thousand is a large number, while zero times a million is still zero. So, this is another secret of the 4%. They always focus on what they have and expect it to multiply, even if it is very small to begin with. The 96% continue to focus on what they don't have and what they can't do, and experience no multiplication whatsoever."

"Let me give you one other example from the Bible," said Papa. "In Second Kings, chapter four, verses one through seven (2 Kings 4:1-7), we read the experience of a widow facing a very severe situation due to debt. Her husband had borrowed money, and thereby made himself a servant to his creditors until the debt was paid. Unfortunately, the man died and left his family to face the creditors. When the creditors then came to collect, they demanded to take this widow's two sons as literal slaves in payment of the debt. The woman cried out to Elisha the prophet for help. The prophet immediately asked her, 'What do you have in the house?' The woman said, 'I have nothing in the house except a jar of oil.'"

"Again, we see that the woman is focused on what she does not have. Elisha did not ask her what she did not have. He asked her what she had. Even when she told him, she had completely discounted the one jar of oil that she had because it was so insufficient. This is how the 96% always think. They don't understand or expect natural or supernatural multiplication. However, the 4%, of which Elisha was one, focus on what is available, and expect multiplication."

"Elisha then instructed the woman to borrow as many jars as she could and to begin to pour the oil from the one jar she had into the other jars. Upon doing so, the woman found that God supernaturally multiplied the oil to fill all the jars she had. Elisha then instructed the woman to sell the multiplied oil, use the money to pay her husband's debt, and then have sufficient left over for her family to live on for some time. So, Isaac, the lesson is this. While the 96% focus on what they don't have and what they can't do, the 4% focus on what they do have and what they can do, and expect God to multiply what they have," concluded Papa.

Isaac then said, "Another thing I have observed about my friends is that they are always stressed out and never have time for anything. I worry about Bill and Sue's marriage. Bill has gotten a second job at night and is never home. Any time I invite him to do anything, he doesn't have time, and seems to live under an incredible amount of emotional stress and pressure in his marriage. Why do you think that is, Papa? I mean, Rachael and I seem to have a very relaxed and peaceful life compared to most of our friends."

Papa began, "Isaac, another consequence of not learning how to invest in things that multiply is a lack of meekness. Let me explain to you what I have learned about meekness. Jesus said in

Matthew 5:5 *'Blessed are the meek, for they shall inherit the land (earth).'* I always thought that meekness was just another word for humility. But I have since learned that humility is an attitude, while meekness is an action. Humility is who I am, while meekness is what I do."

"I further learned, from the Vines Bible dictionary, that meekness is a fruit of power[2]. That dictionary states that Jesus was meek, not because He was impotent, but rather because He voluntarily limited Himself to use only a small percentage of available power. So I have come to define meekness this way: meekness is voluntarily limiting the use of available resources or power. A meek person is one who has great power or resources, but voluntarily limits oneself to use only a percentage of that resource or power. In other words, a meek person is one who lives with margins in life."

> A meek person is one who has great power or resources, but voluntarily limits oneself to use only a percentage of that resource or power.

"Something I realized as I thought about this was the fact that meekness and debt are then opposites. If meekness is having margins, then the opposite is having negative margins. Meekness is having a certain capacity and voluntarily using less than 100%. The opposite would be to have a certain capacity and voluntarily using more than 100% of capacity. The word that describes this choice is debt. So I discovered that meekness and debt are direct opposites. Going back to Matthew 5:5 in the Bible, Jesus said that two things would happen to the meek: they would be blessed,

---

[2] Vine, W.E., Unger, Merrill F., White, William Jr., *An Expository Dictionary of Biblical Words* (Nashville, TN, Thomas Nelson Publishers, 1984), p. 728

and they would inherit the land. So what then would befall the indebted?" asked Papa.

"Probably the opposite," chimed in Isaac. "The indebted would be not blessed, or, I guess, would be cursed, and would not inherit or would lose the land."

"Exactly right," said Papa. Once I understood this, I was then wondering what the practical implication of this was in our modern time. One day last year I was talking with my own father, your grandfather, who lived through the Great Depression years of the 1930s here in the U.S. I was asking him what happened to people financially during the 1930s. He told me that many people lost their houses, farms, cars, and businesses, but that a few people became millionaires during the depression."

"Wondering what was the difference between those who lost everything and those who became millionaires during the '30s, I asked my father why and how people lost their properties and houses. He told me that it was primarily because they were in debt and couldn't make the payments. The bank then repossessed their properties and possessions, and then sold these assets at auction for pennies on the dollar. Who do you think bought them?" asked Papa.

"Probably the people who had a little bit of extra cash and weren't in debt themselves," answered Isaac.

"Exactly right," replied his father. "And what is the term that describes people who have extra cash?"

"THE MEEK!" exclaimed Isaac, excitedly. The light bulb had just gone on for him. "So, what you are saying is that in the 1930s, people who carried debt on their properties, businesses, cars and such lost those things to the bank, and meek people then bought them from the bank. So in this way, the indebted were not blessed and lost the land, and the meek were blessed and literally inherited the land, and cars and businesses, and houses that the indebted had lost. Is that right?"

"Absolutely," replied Papa. "This is probably the reason that many of your friends are so stressed out and frazzled. They are not meek and carry lots of debt. Debt on things that don't multiply leads to poverty, slavery, and lack of peace. Jesus told us a little later in Matthew that if we take His yoke upon us, which is a yoke of meekness, we would be at peace and find rest for our souls. He said exactly:

Matthew 11:28-29

28Come unto me, all ye that labor and are heavy laden, and I will give you rest.

29Take my yoke upon you, and learn of me; for I am meek and lowly in heart: and ye shall find rest unto your souls. 30For my yoke is easy, and my burden is light.

Papa continued, "Jesus here characterizes His yoke as one of meekness and lowliness, or humility of heart. He says that if you take upon yourself, an attitude of humility and a lifestyle of meekness your soul will find rest, your yoke will be easy, and your burden will be light. You can always tell under whose yoke someone is walking by simply asking them or observing whether their life is characterized by the words, "easy and light" or "difficult and heavy." If the yoke on someone's life is difficult and their burden seems to be heavy, then you can be assured that in that particular area they are not meek, and it is not Jesus' yoke that is upon them."

"You know, Isaac," continued Papa, "Meekness does not just apply to finances. It can also apply to time, relationships, or physical health. I have observed a cycle in the lives of many of the 96% thinkers. They start out incurring financial debt. So they are not meek in their money. They then get a second or third job to try to make their payments and now are not meek in their time. They then begin to have no margins in relationships with their wives and children. "

"Frequently when a man starts down this road, he cannot keep his promises to his wife and kids due to his lack of margins in time and money. So he begins to break promises and commitments to the family. Each time he does so, he is incurring a relational debt. His wife may extend him a certain amount of "relational credit," but at some point she tires of excuses for why he doesn't keep his word to her. This can damage or destroy a marriage. Because of the pressure and stress due to no margins in finances, time, or relationship, he is burning the candle at both ends and begins eating poorly, sleeping poorly, and all the while carrying huge amounts of stress. This will eventually take a toll on his physical health, and he may face a serious health challenge. This then requires more money and time to resolve, putting more pressure on his already stretched time and financial resources.

"So, such a man as I just described is living with financial debt, relational debt, time debt, and physical health debt. If he continues in this lifestyle Matthew 5:5 guarantees that he will not be blessed and will lose the "land" of his marriage, his family, his finances, his time, and his health. I believe that Jesus is explaining a principle here. It is not just about money or physical land. In whatever area of life we are indebted and not meek, we will lose the "land" in that area. So this is probably what is happening to several of your friends. Because they are not meek, their yoke is difficult and their burden is heavy in several areas of life. And in these areas, they are in danger of losing their "land.""

"Wow!" exclaimed Isaac. "I hope I can explain this to Bill and Sue. That is exactly what is happening to them. They are in danger of losing their marriage and are always stress out and arguing about money, and time priorities. I hope I can explain to them this understanding of meekness and multiplication."

Secret Number 3 Part 1: Invest only in things that multiply. Never borrow money to purchase a depreciating asset or to invest in something that doesn't increase the value of the asset or cash flow significantly more than the cost of the interest you must pay to borrow the money.

Make sure to have only one Master, God, in your financial life. Live a lifestyle of meekness, and walk with margins in the significant areas of your life.

Reflection

1. Explain how many financial masters you have, and how they affect your life?

2. If you carry debt in your life, what kind of emotional pressure has that debt created for you? What does it feel like?

3. If you are married, how has debt created strife and conflict between you and your spouse?

4. What is your plan to eliminate debt, or if you have no plan, what is your plan to get some help to create a debt elimination plan?

5. Describe things that you have invested in that have multiplied, or things that had the potential to multiply and didn't work out?

6. Describe how you, as a husband (or wife), may have found yourself feeling trapped between your job (making a living) and your family, and sometimes have compromised your word to your family due to financial pressure?

7. In what ways have you found yourself focusing on what you don't have and what you can't do, and how could you change that?

8. What will you now do differently in order to eliminate debt and invest in things that multiply?

CHAPTER 4

INVEST IN MULTIPLIERS

Third Secret: Part 2 –
Invest in People Who Are Multipliers

A second part of this third secret has to do with the people in whom one invests time, money and energy. While the 96% tend to invest in people who are their friends and are nice people, the 4% intentionally invest the majority of their time and energy in people who have the potential to multiply. The 4% frequently use qualification tests to determine the multiplication capacity of those in whom they might invest time, money and energy. The 96% rarely qualify anyone, and usually indiscriminately invest their time, money and energy in non-multipliers.

While the other Wealth Secrets about which we are speaking in this book pertain to anyone, this particular part of the principle pertains specifically to leaders, who are called by God to lead, grow and build an organization, be it a business, a church, or a charity. Realizing that not everyone is called to lead and grow a business or an organization, we see instead that many are called to be part of a team that is growing. In this way, many will accomplish their God-given purpose.

Consequently, those who are called and desire to grow an organization must learn to invest in multipliers, while those who are called to be part of an organization team will be more concerned with accomplishing their function so that the overall team can succeed, grow, and multiply.

Through their early twenty's, Isaac and Rachael continued to build their businesses and gain equity in their real estate holdings. One day Rachael was approached by Julie, one of the other young women from their church congregation about a network marketing opportunity. Rachael and Isaac had both been together with Julie on the overseas missions team in Africa, helping to deliver nutritional food to the malnourished children.

Later after returning home, Julie had discovered that the charity organization that provided the nutrient-dense food supplements to the children in Uganda was actually a charitable outreach arm of a for-profit network marketing company that produced similar nutritional supplements that were marketed in the United States. Julie was very excited about the company, the products they produced, and the business opportunity to generate an additional cash flow. While Rachael had become quite interested as well, Isaac was less than excited when he heard about it from Rachael.

"Rachael," Isaac exclaimed, "you know we have gone to two or three of those multi-level marketing presentations, and they are all the same. People get very excited about the prospect of making money from involving large numbers of people in their business, but there is not really any product that is special or of any unique value."

"Isaac," replied Rachael, "Julie is quite convinced that this company really does have a unique product that makes a significant difference in the quality of life and health of the consumers. You remember the change we saw in the lives of the orphans in Uganda when we added the nutrient-dense supplements to their diets?"

"Yeah, I do," replied Isaac, recalling to mind specific kids he had met on the trip. "That was quite amazing to see the change in their countenances when they received the nourishment their bodies were craving."

"Well, Julie told me several stories recounting similar results with her own family members and friends when they added these nutritional supplements to their diets. If that is true, I can think of many people I know here who need nutritional supplements. Besides, if I could really generate a cash flow from this business, I would love to be able to not only support the kids in Uganda with food, but to actually build and staff a couple orphanages for some of the kids we saw whose parents were AIDS victims."

"My heart really broke when I saw so many little children just living on the streets with no one to care for them. Isaac, we don't have the cash flow currently going into our 'Offerings' jar to do any more than we are now. I have felt in my spirit ever since Julie told me about it, that this business could be God's channel of additional provision to actually do something about the street orphans we saw. Anyway, would you be willing to at least try the products for a couple of months and conduct the due diligence to read up on the product and hear Julie's business coach give a presentation?"

"Sure," replied Isaac, smiling. "The worst that can happen is that it simply turns out to be just another scam, and we'll then decline to participate any further."

Rachael then purchased some the nutritional products. Isaac also did some research on the company, the products and their business plan. After his research and using the products for two months, Isaac was also convinced that this was legitimate business, with a legitimate, unique product. While not having much time personally to divert into building another business himself, Isaac was happy to support Rachael in starting and building this business.

"However," he told Rachael, "Before you really jump into this, I would like for us to get my father's counsel." Rachael heartily agreed. So Isaac made an appointment to talk with his father over dinner again about Rachael's new business idea.

Isaac and Rachael finished the lovely dinner his mother had prepared for them, and adjourned to the family room. Once seated, Isaac and Rachael explained to Papa all the information and experience they had about the network marketing business they had been investigating. Rachael also shared her vision to use the potential additional cash flow to build orphanages in Uganda.

"So Papa, do you think it would be a good idea for Rachael to divert some time and a little money from our investment jar into this business?" Isaac asked. "I don't have much time myself to put into it, but Rachael has time available, and a real passion for helping people improve their health through the benefits provided by the products this company supplies," he added.

Papa paused for a moment, scratching his chin and then began. "Isaac, there are legitimate networking companies with legitimate products, and then there are some that have no real product, but in reality just transfer money from the pockets of many to the pockets of a few. It sounds from what you have shared like this company has legitimate, unique products, with a legitimate sales organization, and compensation plan. If this is true, and Rachael feels called by God to build this business, then there is only one factor missing in order to have her business succeed. She will need people in whom she can invest to help her build her business. I'd like to share with you both one more secret of the 4%. "

"Remember," said Papa, "I told you earlier that the 4% only invest in things that multiply?"

"Yes," replied Isaac.

"Well," continued Papa, "the 4% primarily invest in people who multiply, or at least have the potential to multiply. The 96% spend most of their time, money, and energy investing in people who never multiply at all. Rachael, would you like to become great in business and great in the Kingdom of God?"

"Of course, Papa," replied Rachael.

"The way one becomes great in business is the same way that Jesus said to become great in the Kingdom of God. Whoever serves the most people becomes the greatest in the Kingdom of God. In the business you are contemplating starting, if you find a way to serve more people, you will make more

> Whoever serves the most people becomes the greatest in the Kingdom of God.

money. Whoever serves the most people prospers most. This is how Jesus said it." Papa opened his Bible program and read:

Matthew 20:25-28

25 But Jesus called them to Himself and said, "You know that the rulers of the Gentiles lord it over them, and their great men exercise authority over them. 26 It is not this way among you, but whoever wishes to become great among you shall be your servant, 27 and whoever wishes to be first among you shall be your slave; 28 just as the Son of Man did not come to be served, but to serve, and to give His life a ransom for many."

"So, Rachael," continued Papa, "The more people you learn how to serve, the more you will prosper in the Kingdom of God and in business. In this passage, Jesus talks more about attitude than anything else. Our attitude is to be that of a servant, seeking to bless and prosper others, not to use others to prosper ourselves. If you begin your network marketing business with this attitude, you will prosper naturally, and God will also prosper you supernaturally."

"I want to show you another scripture in which we are told what sort of people to look for in order to be able to serve more people."

2 Timothy 2:2

2 The things which you have heard from me in the presence of many witnesses, **entrust these to faithful men who will be able to teach others also.**

"Here we see, Rachael, Paul was hoping to multiply his message and his work. He therefore was not willing to invest his time and energy indiscriminately. Paul is instructing Timothy, his trainee, as to what type of people he should look for to invest in. He told Timothy to look for a person with two specific qualifications. The first was that he was to look for a person who was faithful, or in other words, a diligent person who would accomplish the tasks given to him."

"However, this was not the only qualification. Paul instructed Timothy to look for someone who was also able to multiply the teaching into others. So Paul is looking for at least three generations of multiplication beyond himself. Paul found Timothy, who apparently met these two qualifications. He was then instructing Timothy to find people who could also multiply into the lives of others."

"You see, Isaac," continued Papa, "there are many people who are faithful, but have no ability to multiply. I have found that most people only look for people who are faithful, but completely disregard the quality of multiplication. I have seen many business people, and pastors or congregational leaders spend lots of their time and energy investing in people who are nice, friendly, and faithful, but have no experience in, or capacity to, multiply. The result is: no growth. So, this is why Paul instructed Timothy to identify and invest in men who are both faithful and know how to multiply at least two generations."

"That makes total sense," said Isaac. "I can see that this same principle applies to all of my other businesses as well."

"I understand the principle of investing in faithful multipliers," said Rachael, "but it seems to me sort of crass and heartless to just dismiss people if they are not multipliers. It seems like you are saying, Papa, that we should not give any time, energy, or money to people who are not productive multipliers. But what about people like Mother Teresa, who gave her whole life, all her time, energy and money to poor, needy, unproductive non-multipliers? Was that not virtuous and a valuable use of money, time, and energy?"

"Excellent point and question Rachael," replied Papa. "I believe the manner in which Mother Teresa lived her life was very virtuous, and valuable. However, I'm not so sure Mother Teresa spent all her time with poor, needy, unproductive non-multipliers, as you said. How many Catholic nuns and other godly missionaries do you think there are around the world giving their lives to the poor and needy as Mother Teresa did in Calcutta, India?"

"I don't know," responded Rachael.

"Probably thousands, wouldn't you think?" asked Papa.

"I suppose," said Rachael.

"Why do you think that Mother Teresa is so well known around the world for her work? Why are none of the many other people doing the same type of work not known?"

"I have no idea," said Rachael.

"There could be many reasons," continued Papa, "but one of the reasons, I believe, is because Mother Teresa reached and served many more of the world's poor than almost anyone else. Let's just take a quick look online and see what is written about her."

Papa opened his iPad and typed into the browser the words "Mother Teresa." One of the first articles to come up was a general article on Wikipedia about Mother Teresa and her work.

"Look here," said Papa as he began to read.

"Mother Teresa's Missionaries of Charity at the time of her death had 610 missions in 123 countries including hospices and homes for people with HIV/AIDS leprosy and tuberculosis, soup kitchens, children's and family counseling programs, orphanages and schools. She received numerous awards including the Indian government's Bharat Ratna in 1980 and the Nobel Peace Prize in 1979."[1]

Papa continued, "Mother Teresa is famous, and, I believe, great in the Kingdom of God, because she served hundreds of thousands or millions of the 'poorest of the poor' through her missionary organization. Remember Jesus' principle that whoever wishes to be great in the Kingdom of God must become servant of all. How did Mother Teresa do this?"

"Apparently," continued Papa, answering his own question, "at some point Mother Teresa realized that in order to serve more people she could not do it all herself. She realized that she would have to multiply her work through others. Had she simply

---

[1] Wikipedia, http://en.wikipedia.org/wiki/Mother_Teresa

continued to spend all of her time and energy only with the poor and needy around her, she would have been very limited in how many people she could serve. So apparently, Mother Teresa began to spend some time and energy recruiting, training, releasing and nurturing others, who could also do the same work with the poor and needy. She must have trained some leaders, some multipliers, and some multipliers of multipliers in order to arrive at the point where she could serve millions of poor and needy people through 610 missions in 123 countries."

"Wow! That is incredible, Papa!" exclaimed Rachael. "I never realized or thought of Mother Teresa as one who invested in multipliers, but in order to lead the type of mission that she did, and reach the numbers of poor that she did, it is obvious that she must have invested in multipliers. And she certainly wasn't crass or heartless. But Papa, most people are not multipliers. Do they have no value? It almost seems like you are saying that multipliers are the only ones who are valued and honored."

"Rachael," said Papa, "the desire and ability to multiply are qualities of leadership. Not everyone is called to be a leader, or a multiplier. I am teaching you this principle because you and Isaac are both called by God to be leaders and multipliers. However, I believe that God measures fruit by teams, as it were, rather than by individuals. Many of the other nuns in Mother Teresa's team are not leaders, and are not called by God to be multipliers. However, each one is just as valuable as the leaders, and the entire team is credited with the harvest. Just as in a sports team, there are leaders and star players who are well known, but without the functioning of the other teammates the team would never win, and the leader would accomplish very little."

> The desire and ability to multiply are qualities of leadership.

"However," continued Papa, "if you are called to build a business, Rachael, then you must learn the skills of leadership, and how to recruit, train, release and nurture other multipliers. If you spend all your time with people who don't multiply, I would suggest that you not try to lead and grow a business. It would be much better for you to be a teammate, rather than a leader, and work in someone else's business. However I don't believe that this is your calling. I believe that God has called and equipped you to lead and multiply."

"I agree, Papa," said Rachael. "I am really excited to learn how to lead and multiply in my business. I now understand that we are not to devalue or discredit people who are not leaders or multipliers, but in order to grow an organization, a leader must focus on the multipliers, or the business won't grow."

"That's exactly correct. You're a quick learner, Rachael," said Papa.

'So, Papa, let me ask another obvious question. You taught us from the Second Timothy passage that a leader should look for people who are faithful and can multiply. How do I find the people who are faithful and can multiply?"

Papa smiled and then opened to another Bible passage on his iPad. "The short answer, Rachael, is that you qualify them. Give them a qualification test to determine their faithfulness and ability to multiply. Let me show you another passage in the Bible in which Jesus told a parable in order to answer this very question. It is found in Luke 19.

Luke 19:12-27

12 So He said, "A nobleman went to a distant country to receive a kingdom for himself, and then return. 13 And he called ten of his slaves, and gave them ten minas and said to them, 'Do business with until I come back.' 14 But his citizens hated him and sent a delegation after him, saying, 'We do not want this man to reign over us.' 15 When he returned, after receiving the kingdom, he ordered that these slaves, to whom he had given the money, be called to him so that he might know what business they had done. 16 The first appeared, saying, 'Master, your mina has made ten minas more.' 17 And he said to him, 'Well done, good slave, because you have been faithful in a very little thing, you are to be in authority over ten cities.' 18 The second came, saying, 'Your mina, master, has made five minas.' 19 And he said to him also, 'And you are to be over five cities.' 20 Another came, saying, 'Master, here is your mina, which I kept put away in a handkerchief; 21 for I was afraid of you, because you are an exacting man; you take up what you did not lay down and reap what you did not sow.' 22 He said to him, 'By your own words I will judge you, you worthless slave. Did you know that I am an exacting man, taking up what I did not lay down and reaping what I did not sow? 23 Then why did you not put my money in the bank, and having come, I would have collected it with interest?' 24 Then he said to the bystanders, 'Take the mina away from him and give it to the one who has the ten minas.' 25 And they said to him, 'Master, he has ten minas already.' 26 I tell you that to everyone who has, more shall be given, but from the one who does not have, even what he does have shall be taken away. 27 But these enemies of mine, who did not want me to reign over them, bring them here and slay them in my presence."

"The first important secret we see in this parable is that the master wanted to invest in people who were faithful, and could multiply. He was looking for people to whom he could grant great authority, and stewardship of great wealth. If one wants to qualify someone to manage a great amount of his wealth and exercise great authority, how would one find and qualify such a person? How about giving several people the management over a small amount of wealth and small authority, and then observe how they do? This is exactly what the master in Jesus' parable did."

Papa continued, "This master was planning to grant authority over several of his newly inherited cities to a few governors. How much is a city worth? We don't know, but probably billions of dollars in today's value. How would he qualify people to identify those who were faithful and could multiply? This master chose ten of his servants as candidates and gave them each a certain amount of his money, called a mina (perhaps something like ten thousand dollars in today's economy)."

"The master neglected to tell any of the candidates that this was a qualification test for a much larger responsibility. Instead, he simply told them to do business with the mina until he returned. Having given them each an assignment (to multiply one mina), he said he would return and hold them accountable for their actions. Apparently, none of the candidates understood that the master had given them the mina as a qualification test. All ten assumed that the master was greedy and simply wanted to use them to multiply the mina for himself."

Papa then said, "I frequently use this same strategy to qualify people in my business. I give them a 'mina' and watch what they do with it. A 'mina' in my terms, is simply a responsibility or opportunity. I then watch to see who is faithful and who can multiply. Rachael, I suggest that you do the same in your new business. I'll explain how in just a minute."

"But first, let's continue on with the story in this passage. When the master returned, he asked for an accounting from his servants."

"The first critical principle we see from this parable is to qualify your candidates. Secondly, never give a candidate a mina without an accountability date. When the master returned he requested to know what had been done with the mina. This first servant, about whom we are told, reported to the master that he had multiplied the one mina ten-fold and had an additional ten minas to give the master. When the master then commended this servant and conveyed authority to him over ten cities, I suspect that the mouths of the other servants and bystanders dropped open, and they probably thought to themselves, 'Cities? Authority over cities? You never said anything about that before. If I would have known you were granting authority over cities I would have worked harder.' Of course! This was the point. The master wanted to know what each candidate would do with money that didn't belong to him without knowing that there were cities at stake. This is the initial test of faithfulness," Papa said.

"The second candidate came and reported that he had multiplied his mina five to one. Again the master commended him and granted him authority over five cities, each being worth billions."

"The third candidate came and reported that he had simply retained the mina in a handkerchief and had done nothing with it. He was now returning it intact. For fear of the master, he had not even tried to increase his mina. So this candidate failed the qualification test on both accounts; he was neither faithful to carry out the assignment nor, able to multiply. The master expressed great displeasure in him and ordered that the mina be taken from him and given to the one who had ten," continued Papa.

"It is interesting to note that we only hear about three of the ten servants, to whom minas were given. What happened to the other seven? Apparently nothing worth noting. If it is like today, probably three of the ten spent the mina and had nothing left to return to the master. The other four may have not only spent it, but then borrowed more money and owed another three minas," exclaimed Papa. "Judging from what the master said to the one who buried his mina in a handkerchief, imagine what he would have said to the three who spent the entire mina, or the four who perhaps spent the mina and even borrowed more?"

"Probably words that were not too pleasant," replied Isaac.

Rachael then summarized, "So if I understand so far, Papa, what you are saying is that in building a business, church, ministry, or any organization of people that I would want to grow, I should do three things:

1.) Have the attitude of a servant, and seek the welfare of those who will receive the benefit of my product or service.

2.) To grow, I should look for people who have two qualities: those who are faithful and can multiply.

3.) I should identify my multipliers by giving many potential candidates a qualification test, and then choose to work with those who prove themselves faithful and can actually multiply.

Is that right?"

"You got it, Rachael," said Papa. "But let me give you two more quick principles we see from the parable. Firstly, don't continue to chase people who say that they will respond, but in actuality they don't. Judge your candidates by their actions, not by their words or good intentions. Many people say that they want to or will do this or that, but never actually do what they say. These are buriers, not multipliers. No matter how nice they are, or if they are your close friends or not, take the mina away from them and give it to your multipliers. This is a mistake the 96% thinkers consistently make in trying to grow any organization."

> Judge your candidates by their actions, not by their words or good intentions.

"Secondly," continued Papa, "we see from the parable that in order to find two true multipliers, the master had to sift through ten people. This is fairly common. In order to find two multipliers, one will usually have to give minas to at least ten people. Many people, not realizing this get discouraged when the majority of people they have hopes for don't respond. If you expect to only find two out of ten who are faithful and can multiply, you will not become angry or discouraged with those who don't respond to your challenge. Rather, you will become excited about the two true multipliers you find from sifting through ten or more to whom you give an opportunity to multiply the mina you give them."

"Thank you so much, Papa," said Isaac. Now that we know how to find and invest in people who will multiply, I think that Rachael can build a prosperous network marketing business with the company and products in which we already believe."

Isaac and Rachael left his parents' house that evening very excited about the potential of Rachael's new nutritional supplement business. At home, Isaac and Rachael continued their discussion together. Isaac started, "Let's quickly write down the principles we learned from my father this evening before we forget.

"Good idea," said Rachael, opening her laptop and her word processing program. "OK, I'll just make a simple list of the scriptures and principles Papa shared with us." Rachael then wrote the following list and read it to Isaac.

Matthew 20:25-28

1. Have the attitude of a servant. He who serves the most people prospers most.

2 Timothy 2:2

2. Invest your time, money, and energy in multipliers who can teach others to multiply. Don't devalue non-multipliers. But if you want to grow spend your quality time with multipliers.

Luke 19:12-27

3. Qualify multipliers by giving minas. Give minas to at least ten candidates, and see what they do with the mina. Be willing to give minas to at least 10 in order to find 2 multipliers.

4. Make sure to give an accountability date to each person and check back with him or her on that

date to see what he or she has done with the mina.

5. If the candidate is faithful with the mina, and shows potential to multiply, engage him/her and invest slowly.

6. It the candidate is faithful with the mina and has already multiplied by the accountability date, rejoice, and invest greatly in him/her.

7. If the candidate buried the mina and has only an excuse on the accountability date, take the mina away from him/her, give it to the one who has multiplied, and don't chase the one who buries. Let him/her go."

Isaac listened as Rachael recited the seven points they had gained from their conversation with Isaac's father. "Excellent," he remarked. "If you follow these seven points, I'm sure your business will grow."

Rachael then continued, "Let's talk for a moment about what kind of a mina I should offer people as I start this new business. As I understand the concept from your father, a mina is an assignment or a challenge we offer people as a qualification test to check their interest level, faithfulness, and ability to multiply, right?"

"I think that is exactly correct," replied Isaac. "In the case of your new business, I think that the best "mina" you can give potential candidates is a business or product presentation mp3 video file online. You can simply give your candidates the web address and ask them for a date by which they can watch the online video. You can then check back on that date to see if they have watched it and if so what their interest level might be."

"That's perfect!" remarked Rachael. "Will you please help me make a list of potential candidates you believe may be interested in joining me in this new business venture? I'd like to start with Bill and Sue. This might really be an answer for them to help solve some of their financial pressure."

"Wow, I think you're right," said Isaac. "Let's contact them tomorrow. I think we should invite Bob, Jim, and their wives too. They each know lots of people and might be really good at this type of business. In terms of friends I know, Aaron, Jacob and Simon also come to mind. I'd be happy to invite them to a meeting if you will organize the presentation."

"Great," said Rachael. "I'm thinking of Sandy, Linda, Cathy, Sarah, Ziva, and Hannah," Rachael chimed in.

By the next morning, Rachael and Isaac had added the names of several more people, who potentially could be interested in Rachael's new venture. Over the next week Isaac and Rachael contacted each of their friends and shared briefly about Rachael's new business. Isaac didn't really know much about the business, so he just made the introduction of each of his friends to Rachael, and let her explain more. Rachael asked each person if he or she would be willing to invest the time to watch the twenty-minute online video presentation. Each of the friends agreed to do so, and gave Rachael an accountability date by which they thought they could complete the assignment. Of course none of them knew that this was Rachael's mina qualification test.

Three days after Isaac and Rachael had spoken with Aaron, about nine thirty in the evening, Isaac's cell phone rang. It was a very excited Aaron on the other end saying, "Hello. I hope I'm not calling too late, Isaac."

"No, not at all. Aaron," replied Isaac. "What's up?"

"Well," continued Aaron, "I watched that online DVD Rachael asked me to watch two evenings ago. I got really excited about the whole idea. But I wondered how some of the other people I know would respond. So, in the last two days, I have gotten ten of my other friends to watch the video. They are all as excited as I am, and we are ready to sign up and get started in building a business. I'm calling to see if you could arrange a meeting as soon as possible with me and my other ten friends to explain more details and register us with your company so we can get our initial product packs and get started."

Isaac, still in shock, mumbled, "Well let me have you talk to Rachael. I think her friend, Julie, can probably conduct a meeting like that."

"Yeah, great," continued Aaron, "but it has to be before Monday next week. I'm going to Miami on Monday, and I have a whole other group of people in mind there to whom I would like to present this business. I will need to get the people here started first and find out how to register the new people I will present to in Miami next week. So, we need to have the meeting as soon as possible this week."

"Okay," said Isaac. "I'll tell Rachael and she'll get hold of Julie and get back with you tomorrow."

When Isaac clicked off his cell phone, he turned to Rachael, still in shock from Aaron's excitement, and exclaimed, "I guess you heard from my end of the conversation that Aaron already had ten others who watched the online presentation.

"Unbelievable," remarked Rachael. "Looks like I already have my first ten-to-one multiplier. And his accountability date is not even for another four days."

The next evening, when Isaac came home for dinner, Rachael met him excitedly at the door and exclaimed, "You'll never guess what happened to me today."

"What?" inquired Isaac.

"Ziva called me this afternoon let me know that she also watched the online video and she already shared it with five of her friends. All five were so impressed that they also want to meet with me to get more information. I immediately called Julie, and it looks like she can meet with all of us Saturday evening."

"Wow! This is incredible. If this continues, you'll probably break some sort of record for the fastest new growth in the company! Did you call Aaron and let him know to invite his group to the meeting on Saturday evening?"

"No, not yet," replied Rachael. "But I will this evening."

Rachael hoped that several others would call with the same type of news as Aaron and Ziva had. However, no one else called. One by one, on the accountability date, Rachael called each of their friends whom she had invited to watch the online presentation. Several had forgotten, but said they would watch it the next week. Three of them had watched it, but said that they really weren't interested. Bill and Sue had watched the presentation and said they were interested. Bob and his wife also watched it and said they needed more information. Both of these couples agreed to attend the meeting that Julie would lead on Saturday evening. James and his wife had watched the presentation and also agreed to come to the meeting on Saturday.

When Saturday came, Aaron excitedly showed up with his group, as did Ziva. While Bill and Sue and Bob and his wife came, James and his wife didn't show up. Several of the others who said that they would attend the meeting did not. While disappointed by the people who said they would attend and did not, Rachael was not discouraged, as she recognized that the invitation to the meeting was simply another qualification test (mina) offered to see who would respond.

The results of the meeting were that both Aaron and Ziva and their groups took off like a shot. They continued offering minas to new people for the purpose of qualification and investing their time and energy in their multipliers. Simon, who also attended that first meeting, caught the vision of the minas and began to qualify his candidates looking for multipliers. Over some time, he also found his multipliers and his business began to pick up momentum. James and his wife did not engage in the business, saying that the initial product pack price was too expensive for them to afford.

Bill and Sue registered and purchased their initial product pack. They left the meeting very excited with a list in their minds of many people they knew that they were hoping to interest in this new business. However, neither Bill nor Sue ever caught the idea of qualifying people to find multipliers. As a result, both Bill and Sue spend countless hours encouraging people to watch the initial online video presentation. Rather than disqualifying those who had excuses why they hadn't watched the presentation, they continued to contact those same people over and over again. They registered a few of their friends, but never did find any multipliers. Consequently, Bill and Sue didn't even make enough money from the business to pay for their own product use, and after nine months of trying, gave up and quit even ordering the product for themselves.

Isaac was heartbroken over Bill and Sue's failure to grow their business, as he had really hoped that Bill and Sue would have been able to significantly supplement their income and relieve some of the financial pressure they had been experiencing. Rachael was also very tempted to continue to chase after Sue and try to help her build her business. However, in the end both she and Isaac realized that Bill and Sue were simply not yet ready to capture the concept of multiplication. No amount of time spent with them would help in that regard.

Over the next couple years, with Isaac's support, Rachael's nutritional supplement marketing business grew to provide an additional six-figure income. Rachael was thrilled because they were able to pour ninety percent of this income into their 'Offerings' jar and use it to begin to build and staff a couple of orphanages in Uganda. Both Isaac and Rachael were able to travel to Africa to help initiate and see this work first hand a couple of times each year.

Meanwhile, Isaac's finance company, car washes, apartment complexes, other real estate holdings and businesses continued to prosper and grow. Consequently, Isaac and Rachael were able to adjust their jars to continually increase the amount available in the 'Offerings' jar to support malnourished children, their African orphanages, and American ministries dedicated to train parents in generational blessing. Besides funding their orphanages, Isaac and Rachael also founded and funded a local charitable ministry, designed to teach teens how to manage and invest money. They took great pleasure in watching young people learn the same secrets that Isaac's father had taught him as a boy growing up.

A year and a half later, Isaac's pastor asked him if he would be willing to help grow a home cell group ministry within the congregation. As they prayed about this challenge, Isaac and Rachael felt that this was something that God wanted them to do. Isaac was asked to pick five other leadership couples within the congregation to begin the ministry. Remembering that Papa had told him, that the same secrets that apply to growing a business work also in growing a church or ministry, Isaac realized that he needed to identify and invest in multipliers in order to start and grow the home cell ministry.

Consequently, he decided to give one hundred couples a mina. Isaac invited all one hundred couples to attend a prayer meeting for the cell ministry to be held at 7:00 AM on a Saturday morning. Only twenty couples showed up to the meeting. Through this mina, Isaac and Rachael began to identify those couples who had a desire, and who were faithful. He then asked each of these twenty couples to invite at least five other couples to another meeting the next Saturday at 7:00 AM. While fifteen of the twenty couples returned the next week, only eight of the twenty were able to envision and motivate others to attend the meeting with them. Now Isaac had identified those eight couples as those who were faithful and could multiply.

Isaac and Rachael began the home cell ministry with these first eight couples as leaders, and the others as assistants. Isaac taught these couples many of the same principles from Matthew 20, Second Timothy 2, and Luke 19 that his father had taught him about identifying and investing in those who are faithful and can multiply. The cell ministry within the congregation began to multiply and prosper prolifically. Under Isaac's leadership, this ministry continued to multiply and became one of the chief factors in growing the congregation for the next several years.

While Isaac and Rachael continued to prosper spiritually, relationally, and financially, unfortunately, Bill and Sue continued to struggle financially just to make their monthly payments. This continued to create relational pressure in their marriage and with their children. They had very little time to pray or pursue their spiritual life. So far this couple had not learned to invest in things that multiply, or to identify and invest in people who are multipliers. Isaac had attempted, through their early twenty's, to share with Bill many times the secrets of the 4% that his father had shared with him. However, somehow, these principles just never seemed to take root in Bill so as to produce any practical change in the way he managed his spiritual, family, or financial life. Isaac and Rachael spent much time in prayer for Bill and Sue and their family.

Secret Number 3 Part 2: Invest money, time and energy in people who are faithful and are multipliers. Give specific qualification tests (minas) to identify faithful multipliers. Then invest in these faithful multipliers, and do not invest time, money, or energy in those who fail the test or don't respond to the opportunity given.

Reflection

1. Describe in what areas of your life you are called to be a leader, and in what areas you are called to be part of a team that someone else leads.

2. Describe in what areas of your life or business you have learned to become a servant to more people and what have been the results?

3. What experiences have you had being faithful and multiplying minas given to you by others? What have been the results?

4. What experiences have you had investing in other people who are multipliers? What have been the results? What strategies did you use to qualify, train, release and nurture these multipliers?

5. What qualification tests (minas) have you learned to use with your children in your family, or in your business? What have been the results?

6. In what areas of your life, business, or ministry do you feel called to invest in multipliers, and what is your plan to do so?

7. How would your life, business, or ministry be different if you invested in multipliers in the areas in which you feel called to do so?

CHAPTER 5

ANTICIPATE ECONOMIC CYCLES

The fourth secret that the wealthy 4% practice and teach their children is to understand, anticipate and prepare for economic cycles. While the 96% tend to think that the economy is linear and will continue to be in the future, the way it has been in the past, the 4% understand that any economy expands and contracts in cycles. Thus the 4% understand that the future may be quite different than the past, as we move into a new phase in the cycle. Financial strategies that have worked in the past may not work in the future, and must be adjusted to accommodate a shift into the next phase of the economic cycle. While the 96% only know how to prosper in a growing economy, the 4% have learned how to prosper equally in times of economic expansion, recession or even depression.

> The 4% have learned how to prosper equally in times of economic expansion, recession or even depression.

Throughout his twenty's, Isaac continued to accumulate rental properties, and grow his finance and other businesses. At the same time, Rachael, with Isaac's support, grew her nutritional supplement marketing business to become one of the top fifty distributors in her company. Since Isaac and Rachael were both born in 1977, they just hit 30 years old in 2007.

In the late fall of that year, Isaac's father called him one day and said, "Isaac, there is something I've been thinking quite a bit about recently that I would like to discuss with you. Would you and Rachael be available for dinner this weekend?"

"Sure," replied Isaac.

After a delicious dinner, prepared by Isaac's mom the next Saturday evening, Isaac and Rachael adjourned with Papa to the living room.

"What's up Papa?" inquired Isaac, taking a sip of his mother's perfectly brewed coffee.

"Isaac," started Papa, "over the last few months, I've been studying some historical charts of the U.S. stock market. At the same time, in my regular daily Bible reading, I came across God's command to ancient Israel to practice the year of Jubilee every fifty years recorded in Leviticus 25. To cut to the chase, I believe that we are about to experience a significant downturn in the U.S. economy, and maybe in the global economy. I believe that you may need to reevaluate your current business strategy."

"Really?" exclaimed Isaac. "Explain to us what you are thinking. "

"In studying the charts I mentioned," started Papa, "it appears to me that over the last few decades, individuals, companies, and even municipal and state governments have taken on an unsustainable amount of debt. I think it is inevitable that sometime soon we will enter into a season of deflation and an elimination of the debt. This will probably happen over a few years' time, but as it does I believe that the value of both residential and commercial real estate will dramatically fall."

Papa continued, "In Leviticus 25, God commanded Israel to declare a year of Jubilee every fifty years. I noticed in this chapter that the following three things were to occur in the year of Jubilee:

1) All debt was to be cancelled or forgiven;

2) All slaves were to go free; and

3) All property was to be given back to the original owner."

"As I studied this chapter on Jubilee, I was asking God the question as to why He commanded Israel to do this. It occurred to me that God, being very smart, realized that whenever credit was made available in any society, human nature dictates with one hundred percent certainty, that over a few decades, people will borrow more money than it is possible to pay back. Additionally, lenders, because of greed, will lend to uncreditworthy borrowers. As a result, over about five decades, or fifty years, the economy in that society will take on an unsustainable amount of debt, and there is a need to eliminate that debt. This is why God commanded Israel to declare a national debt purge every fifty years called Jubilee. Jubilee is a debt reset button, as it were."

"Yeah, but what happens if an economy like ours has no Jubilee, debt purge mechanism?" asked Isaac.

"I was wondering this same thing," replied Papa. "It seems that if an economy has no planned Jubilee, then that economy will have, what I think of as an 'unplanned Jubilee.' As I looked at historical market charts and read some financial articles describing the U.S. and European economies, I noticed that the economy has tended to have a significant deflationary depression approximately every seventy to eighty years. While these deflationary depressions seem to last only about four to five years on the way down, the economy remains flat without much growth for at least another decade or more."

Papa continued, "Obviously the last Jubilee, debt purge in our country happened in the 1930s and was called the 'Great Depression.' About seventy years before that, there was in the U.S. what was known as the 'Panic of 1857,' which was triggered, as I have read, by the failure of the Ohio Life Insurance and Trust Company. This event apparently wasn't deep enough to purge all the debt in the system, and only sixteen years later, in 1873 the U.S. economy entered what was known as the 'Long Depression.' Wild and rampant borrowing, and speculation in the railroads of the time, triggered both the 1873 and 1857 events. In all three of these events (1857, 1873, and 1929), the stock market plummeted dramatically, real estate and commodity prices fell through the floor, and foreclosures and unemployment went through the roof."

"As I was reading about the past depressions in our country, I suddenly realized that exactly the same three things were happening, involuntarily in these deflationary depressions, as God commanded for Israel to enact voluntarily in the Jubilee. Debt was being eliminated or forgiven through foreclosure and defaults on loans. We haven't had actual slaves in our country in the last one hundred fifty years, but we do have people whose whole lives are controlled by creditors, who are in reality debt-slaves. These debt-slaves are set free in the depression through bankruptcy. When people can't pay for a house, car or property they default, and the property then reverts back to the original owner, usually to a bank, through repossession. So in summary in a deflationary depression three things happen:

1) Debt is cancelled or forgiven through default and foreclosure;

2) Debt-slaves are set free through bankruptcy;

3) Properties revert back to the original owner through repossession."

"The primary difference," continued Isaac's father, "between Biblical Jubilee and a modern depression, is that the Biblical Jubilee was meant to be fair and just for all because the timing was planned, declared and known to all. Business deals could be structured according to the number of years left until Jubilee. A modern deflationary depression, on the other hand, is not planned, and catches many by surprise. Many people unjustly lose their businesses, properties or houses because they are unaware that the end of a 70 or 80-year inflationary cycle is at hand. Not realizing that upwards of 70 years of price appreciation is about to be erased in less than 5 years, unwary people buy businesses or real estate at an inflated bubble price only to lose most of their equity value in a very short time."

"Isaac and Rachael," said Papa with a concerned look on his face, "from my study and prayer, I suspect that we are about to enter into another deflationary depression cycle within the next year or two. However, this time, because of the interconnection of the global economy, the debt crisis and ensuing deflation won't be confined to just one nation, but will affect most nations at once. It will for sure affect the United States and Europe."

"Papa," responded Isaac, "it is interesting that you are sharing this with us today. Just this morning in my regular devotion time, I was reading from the book of First Chronicles, chapter twelve in the Bible, and I was impressed to meditate on verse 32."

Isaac opened his iphone Bible program and read:

I Chronicles 12:32

Of the sons of Issachar, men who understood the times, with knowledge of what Israel should do...

Isaac continued, "I shared this passage with Rachael, and the two of us prayed just this morning that we might be sons of Issachar, people who have understanding of the times, and know what to do. Now you are sharing this information with us and I am thinking that this is a specific answer to the prayer we prayed just this morning. If what you are saying is true, and we are about to enter a once in almost a century deflationary depression after 80 years of inflation and price appreciation, that would certainly be critical information to have. So what else has God shown you about this coming involuntary Jubilee as it were, and what practical steps should be taken?" asked Isaac.

"The sad thing that I have realized, Isaac," said Papa, "is that most people are linear thinkers. Most believe that the economy flows in a straight line, while in actuality it is cyclical. Many people fail to see this because the period of the cycles is longer than their entire lifetime. So, many think that what they have experienced economically for the last fifty years will simply continue unchanged. If one did not live through the last depression cycle in the 1930's, it is difficult to believe that we could experience a similar debt purge cycle now."

> Many think that what they have experienced economically for the last fifty years will simply continue unchanged.

"For more than fifty years we have experienced continual price inflation. So, even financial advisors will show clients fifty years of data, to convince them that the past trend will continue into the future. However, in my opinion, it is the wrong fifty years. The fifty years from 1957 to 2007 doesn't include a debt purge cycle. The data from 1900 to 1950 would tell an entirely different story because it includes the debt reset part of the cycle in the middle. I am convinced that we are about to enter another debt purge cycle resulting in massive deflation, and a huge drop in real estate prices, commodity prices and equity prices. I would not at all be surprised to see a drop in the Dow Jones Average again sometime within the next 12 to 18 months at least as large as the 1929 stock market crash of 49%."

"Let me show you a couple of charts that appear to affirm this conclusion. The Dow Jones Industrial Average is a good measure of our U.S. stock market overall. As you can see, the curve is on a slow upward climb from the 1940s through the 1980s. Then in the 1980's the curve inclines significantly upward and in the 1990s the curve begins to climb upward at an acute angle. We see a drop during the nine - eleven crisis in 2001 lasting into 2002 and then a steep climb through the 2000s until now."

"If you look at the second chart that shows data from 1927 through 1933, you see a similar climb in the curve during the "Roaring 20's. This economic surge upward was rudely interrupted by the stock market crash of 1929, which signaled the beginning of the Great Depression, or debt reset cycle. The steeply upward climbing curve from the chart in the 1920's looks very similar to me to the current chart of the 2000's. Because I believe that the economy moves in cycles that go up and down, rather than in a straight line that only goes up, I suspect that the peak of the curve we are seeing now at the end of 2007 is parallel to the peak we saw in the autumn of 1929."

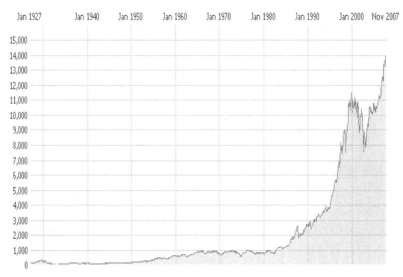

http://moneycentral.msn.com/

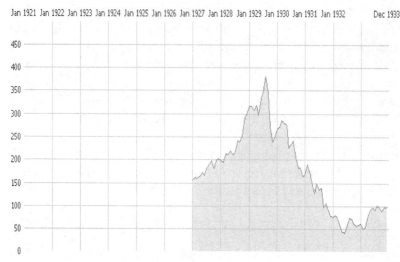

Jan 1921 Jan 1922 Jan 1923 Jan 1924 Jan 1925 Jan 1926 Jan 1927 Jan 1928 Jan 1929 Jan 1930 Jan 1931 Jan 1932   Dec 1933

http://moneycentral.msn.com/

"Wow, Papa," exclaimed Isaac, with Rachael nodding in hearty agreement. "That is incredible. My head is spinning at the moment with a million questions."

Rachael piped up, "Papa, do you remember the conversation we had a few years ago when we were talking about the idea that the wealthy 4% only invest in things that multiply?"

"Yes," replied Papa.

"You told us in that conversation," continued Rachael, "that back in the Great Depression of the 1930's many people lost everything, but a few people became multi-millionaires. You said that the people who became millionaires were the meek, who had a little bit of extra cash, and were not in debt. While people in debt lost their farms, properties, houses, businesses and cars to foreclosure and repossession by the bank, the meek with a little extra cash then bought these things from the bank for pennies on the dollar. So would one of the secrets of the wealthy 4% be to anticipate not only economic booms, but also economic downturns and make sure to be out of debt and financially meek before the Jubilee, debt reset cycle begins?"

"Absolutely!" exclaimed Papa. "Excellent insight, Rachael," he replied, taking a sip of his coffee. "You're already ahead of me. The ones who became millionaires in the 30's were indeed the financially meek, who were out of debt, had extra cash, and thus were on the correct side of the wealth transfer equation."

"The wealth transfer equation?" asked Isaac. "You have never mentioned that before. What is it?"

"Well," replied Papa. "This is an equation we find in the book of Proverbs in the Bible. Proverbs 13:22 tells us that *'the wealth of the wicked is stored up for the righteous.'* This verse talks about a transfer of wealth. The negative side of the wealth transfer equation is the side from which the wealth is being transferred, while the positive side is that side to which the wealth is being transferred. Upon reading this, I wanted to make sure that I was on the receiving side of this transfer equation."

"I've heard of that scripture and we heard a message by a guest speaker at our church teaching on the coming wealth transfer," said Rachael. "He told us that since we were new creations in Christ, according to 2 Corinthians 5:17-21 we have *'become the righteousness of God in Him.'* Therefore we are qualified as "the righteous' and according to Proverbs 13:22, we can expect to receive much wealth being transferred from the wicked in the coming days."

Papa then asked, "How do you think that the wealth might transfer in practical reality? Will extra money supernaturally appear in your bank account? Or will wicked people be motivated to give you their properties and wealth, or what?"

"No, probably not either of those ways," replied Rachael.

"I believe that there is a little more to the wealth transfer equation than what you have heard," continued Papa. "Many times God is very practical. Of course, I realize that we are righteous because we have entered into the New Covenant, and

103

as such God sees us as righteous through the shed blood of Jesus the Messiah. But I wanted to know God's definitions of righteous and wicked expressed in the Bible pertaining to money and wealth, not standing before God, sexual morality, or eternal salvation. So I entered the words righteous and wicked into my Bible computer program to see if there were definitions of these words in Scripture. The first reference I came across regarding finances where both words are used was in Psalm 37:21."

Papa turned to that passage in his electronic Bible program and read:

Psalm 37:21-22

21 The wicked borrows and does not pay back, But the righteous is gracious and gives. 22 For those blessed by Him will inherit the land, But those cursed by Him will be cut off.

Papa continued, "I was quite surprised by these scriptural definitions. But when I plugged them back into the wealth equation of Proverbs 13:22 the two sides of the equation were quite clear. Using these definitions, Proverbs 13:22 then says:

'The wealth of the one who borrows and does not pay back (wicked) is stored up for the one who is gracious and gives (righteous).'"

"Wow!" responded Isaac, as the light bulb was coming on for him again. So what you are saying is that **back in the 1930's what your father experienced and described was a wealth transfer.** Houses, farms, businesses, cars were lost by those who were in debt, who had borrowed money to purchase those assets and couldn't make the payments. The banks repossessed those assets, and the meek, who had a little extra cash, bought those same assets from the bank at auction for pennies on the dollar. So that was the practical mechanism of how the wealth transferred from the indebted to the meek."

104

Rachael now excitedly chimed in, "So what happened in the 1930's really was a Proverbs 13:22 wealth transfer!"

"Yes," Papa exclaimed.

Rachael continued, "So it was a fulfillment of Proverbs 13:22 and of the meekness equation we talked about a few years ago from Matthew 5:5, 'Blessed are the meek, for they shall inherit the land.' So combining these three scriptures, Psalm 37:21, Proverbs 13:22 and Matthew 5:5, I see that the meek, because they have extra money in hard times, can be gracious and give. They are blessed and inherit the land, which is also what the next verse in Psalm 37, verse 22 says. On the other hand, the indebted have borrowed and cannot pay back. Without realizing it, they have qualified themselves to be on the negative side of the wealth transfer. In difficult times, they are stretched to the gills, and even if they want to, they cannot be gracious and give. So they lose their wealth and their land as it is transferred to the meek, who are gracious and give."

"You got it," said Papa. "Furthermore, as I studied economic history, I have become convinced that there always is a massive wealth transfer in every unplanned Jubilee economic reset. This was the case in Europe in many past centuries, and in the mid 1800 in the U.S and again in the 1930's. Every 70 to 80 years, it seems that an unsustainable amount of debt must be purged from the economy, and in that process, there is always a huge wealth transfer. Wealth always goes from the indebted to the financially meek."

> There always is a massive wealth transfer in every

"And you believe from your study of the Bible, market charts, and economic history that we are about to enter into another unplanned Jubilee season, or depression soon?" asked Isaac.

"Yes," emphatically stated Papa. "We are now near the end of 2007, and I believe that we could see it begin sometime within the next 12 to 18 months. The deflation cycle may start with the collapse of the housing market and the closure of some significant financial institutions. From top to bottom, the deflationary economic decline usually lasts four to five years. It never goes straight down, but if we look at the chart I showed you before of the 1930's depression we see that the market zigzagged down over four years. There were some significant rallies back up during that time."

"Each time the economy surged back upward, the government and news media always proclaimed that the worst was over and the economy was now recovering, only to have it again drop more precipitously than before. After the second or third rally back and drop is when people on Wall Street started jumping out of windows. Many were fooled with each false recovery. Unfortunately, the cycle does not stop until all the accumulated debt is purged from the economy. The injustice and uncertainty of an unplanned Jubilee debt purge is why I believe that God commanded ancient Israel to plan for and carry out a voluntary Jubilee every fifty years."

"So what should we do to prepare for this next economic season?" asked Isaac. "Of course we have no personal debt or mortgage on our own home. But we do carry quite a bit of debt on some of our rental properties, car wash businesses, and apartment buildings."

"Firstly," said Papa, "recognize that when this deflation cycle ensues, the equity value of your real estate may decline to be a small percentage of its current value. So since you have no debt on your personal residence, if you consider your house a home you want to remain in for at least a couple of decades, and you don't mind watching it's value decline sharply then keep it. If you consider your house an investment and you want to preserve equity value, I suggest that you sell it now, while the housing market is still very strong. If you do so, then rent for four to five years and plan to repurchase a similar house for perhaps only a percentage of the price you sold it for now."

Isaac was doing some quick calculations in his head, understanding what Papa was telling him. "So for example," he said, "We could perhaps sell our house for $500,000 in the next few months. We could then rent a house for perhaps $2,000 per month, or $24,000 per year for five years. That would be $120,000 in rent over five years. So $500,000 minus the $120,000 paid rent would leave us with $380,000 cash to purchase a new home in five years. If you are correct and deflationary depression has made the value of our current house only a percentage of its current value, we could then purchase a similar or nicer house for anything less than $380,000 and still have cash left over. Alternatively, we could keep the house we have now and in five years we would have a house worth significantly less and have no extra cash. Is that what you are saying, Papa?"

"Yes, that is what I believe could be the scenario, Isaac."

Isaac looked at Rachael. He knew that she loved their house and had it fixed up just the way she liked it. He told Papa, "Rachael and I will have to pray about it, but we don't really consider our personal residence as a part of our financial portfolio. It is our home, and since we have no mortgage and plan to live in it for another twenty years at least, we will probably keep it. But I can see what a nightmare the coming deflation could be for people who have a mortgage on their home. Someone could have a home like ours with at least a $400,000 mortgage on it and have the equity value decline to only $100,000 or $200,000. I can see how many people could easily lose their homes in the coming deflationary cycle. I hope we can warn some of our friends who have mortgages on their homes."

"Yes, you are right," said Papa. "Let's talk about your rental properties. The main reason I wanted to talk with you and Rachael is that I think you should consider selling all your rental houses and real estate. You have gained what I believe will be the maximum amount of equity in this current inflation cycle. I don't think you want to hold them any longer and watch the equity value deplete out from under you.

I want to make sure that you and Rachael are on the positive side of the wealth transfer equation. Even though as the housing market declines, the market for apartment rentals will increase, the decline in equity value of those apartment buildings may far outweigh the monthly cash flow to be gained from the rental income. Let someone else take the risk on the equity during the next economic season. Besides, you can get top dollar for those properties at the moment. I don't think you'll see these prices again for at least twenty five to thirty years."

"So, the first obvious point is to eliminate all debt. Somehow many church people have thought that when the Jubilee comes, all debt is forgiven and they get to keep all the stuff. NO! When Jubilee comes, all debt is forgiven, but all the stuff, including houses, goes back to the lender. So the worst situation to be in when the economy turns the corner from an inflation cycle to a debt purging deflation cycle is to be in debt. If you remain in that situation, you become the one from whom the wealth transfers."

Papa," inquired Isaac, "these are all defensive strategies to preserve capital. Can you share with us some offensive strategies to prosper in the coming deflationary depression?"

"Sure," said Papa. "I was just coming to that. For the sons of Issachar, who have eyes to see, this coming season could be the opportunity of a lifetime. If I am right, this could be a unique period of a few years that will only take place one time in your lifetime. You are too young to have experienced the last deflation in the 1930's and you will probably not live long enough to see another one, if the Lord doesn't return for another 80 years."

"Firstly, since you have no personal debt and are cash rich, just hold onto your cash through the next few years. As the economy deflates and the indebted lose their businesses, farms, houses, properties, etc. you will be able to purchase properties and businesses for pennies on the dollar. If you are meek and have cash, you will be a beneficiary of the wealth transfer that will take place in the next few years."

"Another proverb that comes to mind is recorded in Proverbs 30:25." Papa again read:

Proverbs 30:25

25 The ants are not a strong people, but they prepare their food in the summer;

"Ants are creatures that understand seasons. They realize that they must accumulate food in the summer season, in order to be able to survive in the winter season. This reminds me of a friend of mine whose family owns a large conglomerate business in Brazil. My friend's father was a Japanese immigrant to Brazil in the 1930's. As a young man, this new immigrant saw an opportunity to develop technology and began a business that grew substantially, and has become over a six hundred million dollar per year business some seventy years later."

Papa continued, "I was asking my friend recently how his father was able to sustain the business through all the economic turmoil of hyperinflation, and severe depression that has hit Brazil over the last seventy years. My friend basically explained to me that his father was a very wise and very meek man. He actually had prospered in the deflationary depression times more than in the inflationary, high growth times. Really, I think that he prospered because he was one of the 4% thinkers. He understood cycles and prepared for each succeeding cycle."

"When everyone else was taking on debt and rapidly expanding, my friend's father was expanding less rapidly. Others thought that he was too conservative and was missing out on opportunities. But in reality, he was an ant, storing in the summer and realizing that winter was coming. Then when the deflationary debt purge came, this man had no debt and was cash rich. While all his competitors were just struggling to keep their doors open, he was doing fine.

Then in the midst of the worst time, he often lowered his prices and undercut all his competition. Several of his competitors could not sustain their business through the economic deflation time and lost their businesses and equipment to their lenders. My friend's father would then pick up the market share from those competitors and also purchase their equipment for pennies on the dollar. Because he was meek, this man was a beneficiary of the wealth transfer in each of the economic downturns in his country."

"Using this wisdom he would then come out of each economic deflation time with greater market share and increased sales. Because he took a long-term approach to business, understood, anticipated and prepared for each succeeding cycle of the economy, he was able to prosper in each season and use the winter seasons to his advantage. This is how this young Japanese immigrant continued to grow his company over decades of time. I suggest that you do the same in your businesses, Isaac. Unfortunately, most people will not understand or anticipate the coming deflationary debt purge season in our economy."

"Secondly," continued Papa, "most people only know how to invest their money in funds and financial instruments that increase in value as the markets or economy go up. However, few people seem to know how to invest in financial instruments that are leveraged to move the opposite of the stock market or the real estate market. Money can be made when the market moves in either direction. I suggest that you place some small amounts of Risk Capital from your 'Investment' jar in some of these instruments. Remember that Risk Capital by definition is money that you could afford to lose. If I am right, they will greatly increase in value as the economy deflates."

"Thirdly, I have read that historically deflationary depression seasons are incubators for new ideas and technology. Business is not expanding, and people begin spending more time and energy in technology development. So the next few years may be the time to look at investing in the development of new, disruptive technologies."

"Thank you so much, Papa," said Isaac. "Rachael and I will pray about the timing of all we have learned from you today and make our plan to take swift action to eliminate all of our business debt. I now see that the reason you suggested fifteen years ago that I borrow money to invest in real estate was because we were in a growing, inflating economy. The reason we should now sell those properties and eliminate the debt is because we are heading into a deflating contracting economy. What an incredible insight to understand these economic cycles."

"Thanks so much Papa," said Rachael, "for sharing your wisdom with us. You are not only a wonderful father, but also an incredible mentor! You, yourself are obviously one of the sons of Issachar who understands the times and knows what Israel should do. Thanks again."

Isaac and Rachael went home and over next few days, they prayed about each of their properties and businesses. As Papa had suggested, they placed on the market for sale every one of the properties on which they had taken a loan. They determined that Rachael's network marketing business may decline in volume in the coming years, but that they would simply budget for a lesser cash flow from that business for a season. They also determined that they might need to prepare for a much-increased rate of default in Isaac's finance business. However, since Isaac was the lender and not the borrower, he was the one to whom the property he had financed would revert to in the case of default. They would simply need a plan to liquidate more of the items upon which people may default."

As they prayed, Isaac and Rachael also decided to increase the percentage of their cash flow into their Savings jar, reduce the percentage in the current 'Investing' jar and store cash to prepare to purchase the properties and businesses that may be available for pennies on the dollar over the next decade.

Throughout the end of 2007 and early part of 2008, Isaac and Rachael were able to sell all of their business assets on which they had carried debt. Of course they placed ten percent of the increase on each of their properties in their 'Tithe' jar and gave it away. They placed the majority of the balance in their 'Savings' jar to use to purchase new businesses and properties over the next several years in case the equity value of these assets significantly declined, as Isaac's father had thought they would.

As Isaac and Rachael were very busy over the holiday season that year, they didn't have much time to meet with many of their friends. However, Bill and Sue invited them to dinner in January and said they were very excited to share some news with them.

As they sat down to the dinner table with Bill and Sue, Bill opened the conversation, "You know Isaac how you have been sharing with me for several years financial principles that your father has taught you. Unfortunately, it has taken a long time for me to really grasp and implement any of them. However, over the last couple of years, Sue and I have finally understood the secret of putting money in jars and investing in things that multiply. We have actually saved up enough money in our 'Investment' jar to follow you on a small scale."

Pulling up a photo on his ipad, Bill excitedly presented Isaac a picture of a house and proudly announced, "We just closed on this house, with almost nothing down, and already have several perspective tenants to rent it. We're finally investing in something that multiplies!"

Isaac and Rachael glanced at each other with a concerned look. They were both thinking, "How do we tell them what Papa has just shared with us about economic cycles?" It looked to them like Bill and Sue had bought a rental house at the peak of the market and were taking a huge risk of having the equity value decline out from under them.

Over the next couple of hours, Isaac and Rachael tried to share with Bill and Sue about the potential coming season of economic deflation and debt elimination. However, Bill and Sue were so excited about the purchase of their new rental house that they were not persuaded to sell it. They also let Isaac and Rachael know that they had received some inheritance money from a grandparent and had been working with an investment broker from Lehman Brothers to help them invest their inheritance money.

Isaac again warned his friends that based on what they had learned from Isaac's father, perhaps this was not the right time to invest their money in the stock market. However, Bill became a little miffed, and exclaimed, "Isaac, it seems like nothing we do is ever right in your sight. My investment advisor showed me fifty years of history demonstrating that the markets he has our money invested in always come back, even after a significant drop. I don't see why you have to rain on our parade, every time we do anything. We thought you'd be excited for us. But instead all you can do is criticize us."

Both Isaac and Rachael thought it better not to try to explain any further to Bill and Sue. They simply apologized for making their friends feel that they didn't accept or appreciate them. They then congratulated Bill and Sue on their new house purchase and left for home.

Secret Number 4: Understand that the economy is cyclical, not linear. Therefore, always anticipate and prepare for the next phase of the economic cycle. Learn how to prosper equally when the economy is contracting as you do when the economy is expanding.

Reflection

1. In what phase of the economic cycle is the current economy in your region, and what preparations have you made in anticipation of the next phase of the cycle?

2. What people have you known in your life, who understood economic cycles and anticipated and prepared for past cycles? What was the result of their preparation?

3. On which side of the Proverbs 13:22 wealth transfer equation are you currently positioned, and what changes do you see you may need to make in order to move or stay on the correct side of the wealth transfer?

4. What people do you know who lived through the 1930's depression and what insights have they shared with you regarding their experiences?

5. Understanding the difference between Core Wealth and Risk Capital, what steps have you taken to preserve the principle of your Core Wealth, and what strategies has God shown you to potentially multiply your Risk Capital in the upcoming economic season?

CHAPTER 6

LEAVE AN INHERITANCE FOR TWO GENERATIONS

Let's now look at the fifth secret that the wealthy 4% understand and teach their children. This principle is expressed in Proverbs 13:22: *"A good man leaves an inheritance to his children's children."* While the 96% struggle just to pay their own bills and leave a small inheritance to their children, the 4% think generationally and leave a significant legacy and inheritance for at least two subsequent generations.

As 2008 unfolded, Isaac and Rachael were extremely glad that Isaac's father had warned them about the potential shift in the economic cycle. They had eliminated all debt, all investment real estate, had taken their investment and retirement capital out of the stock market, and simply stored it in cash. As a result, Isaac and Rachael were not negatively affected by the crash in real estate prices or the stock market. As Papa had predicted, in 2008, the Dow Jones Industrial Average actually fell just over 50%. This was an even a greater drop than the 49% drop in the market crash of 1929. However, it seemed that most people did not recognize this as the beginning of a new deflationary phase in the economy.

Unfortunately, Bill and Sue lost most of their inheritance money in the collapse of Lehman Brothers in September of 2008. When they asked their broker why he didn't warn them about the possibility of such a market drop and collapse of Lehman Brothers, he simply stated, 'Who could have known? No one could have seen this coming.'

Of course Bill and Sue remembered that Isaac and Rachael had tried to warn them, and Isaac had said that his father was predicting such a downturn. So apparently, not everyone was surprised. Bill and Sue were now kicking themselves for having not listened to their friends back in the beginning of the year. To make matters worse, the equity value of both their own house and their rental house had dropped more than 30% over the last year. In early 2009, Sue suggested that perhaps it would be good to get together with Isaac and Rachael again and see what further advice they might have for the future.

Bill contacted Isaac and asked if they could have dinner again. Isaac said, "You know, Bill, Rachael and I will be having dinner with my parents this Saturday evening. Why don't you join us at my parent's home? I'd like for you to meet my father and ask him some of your questions."

"That would be great," remarked Bill. "What time should we be there?"

"How about 6:00 PM?" said Isaac.

"Great," replied Bill. "We'll see you then."

The following Saturday Bill and Sue joined Isaac and Rachael and his parents for dinner. After the sumptuous meal, they all adjourned to the living room. Bill promptly asked Isaac's father how he knew in advance about the housing and stock market declines. Papa spent the next hour and a half reviewing with Bill and Sue many of the same charts and principles about the biblical Jubilee and coming season of deflation and debt purge.

Bill then asked, "So Mr. Berman, what do you think will happen in the economy over the next couple of years?"

"Good question, Bill," said Papa. "I suspect that we are in for a series of zigzag moves to the downside in the equities and commodities markets. Most people don't realize that in the last depression, the market did not go straight down. Let me show you a chart I recently copied out of an article about the 1930's depression."

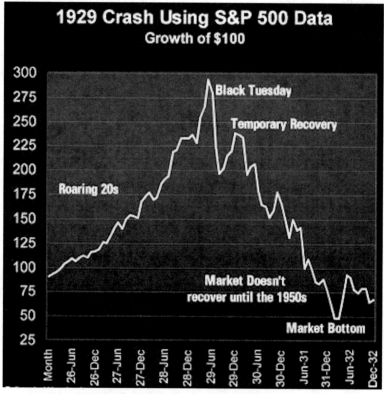

Remembering The 1929 Stock Market Crash

By Antonio Costa on June 28, 2008

http://www.dailymarkets.com/stock/2008/06/28/remembering-the-1929-stock-market-crash/

"You can see from this chart," continued Papa, "that the market actually stair stepped down over several years. I suspect that we will follow the same pattern in this current debt purge cycle. I wasn't sure a year and a half ago exactly when this cycle would start, but I was pretty certain that it would be sometime in 2008 or 2009. Obviously, I was right, and I suspect that we won't reach the bottom of the cycle until sometime in 2013 or 2014. The danger is that we will probably see several strong upsurges in the stock market and the economy on the way down, just the same way they did back in the early 1930's. This is perilous because on each rally back, many people do not recognize that there is a long way yet to go to reach the bottom and jumping back into the market, they are devastated when it turns again and descends lower than before."

"Have a look at this next chart. It depicts the huge initial drop in the market that we have experienced so far. I am expecting a very large rally back with a series of sharp declines and surges back up again over the next few years. I expect a similar pattern to the one from the 1930's. I have no idea where these markets will bottom out, but if the current unplanned Jubilee is similar to the one in the 1930's, we could land with real estate prices in major cities like ours declining by a huge percentage of their peak values last year. This means that in some cities one could buy a similar house to the one he now owns in a few more years for perhaps a fraction of its 2008 value. The stock market could decline as much as 75 to 90% from its peak if it were to repeat what happened in the 1930's," said Papa. "If that takes place, we probably won't see prices recover for at least a couple of decades, well into the 2020's," Papa continued.

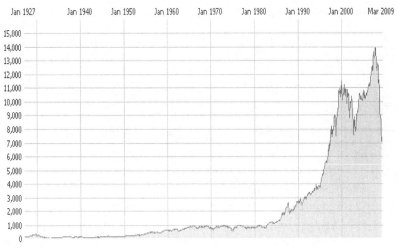

Jan 1927   Jan 1940   Jan 1950   Jan 1960   Jan 1970   Jan 1980   Jan 1990   Jan 2000   Mar 2009

http://moneycentral.msn.com/

Both Bill and Sue were turning pale. "So what do you think we should do with the houses we own with mortgages that are already much greater than the current value of the houses. We are upside down on both of our mortgages."

Papa mused for a moment and then kindly said, "You will need to pray about it and get clear direction from the Lord. However, you might consider selling them both now, and simply take your losses at this point, otherwise you risk losing both of them to the bank as equity values continue to decline."

Bill looked at Isaac and said, "You sure were blessed to never need to take out a mortgage even on the very first house you purchased right out of high school. But how on earth would normal people like us, who don't have a father like yours ever buy a house without needing to borrow money from a bank?"

Papa continued, "A few years ago I explained to Isaac a secret that our family and many in our community have practiced for centuries. In our community, each generation has always felt a responsibility to help the next two generations get started. This principle comes from Proverbs 13:22 in the Bible. It says:

119

Proverbs 13:22

22 A good man leaves an inheritance to his children's children,

And the wealth of the sinner is stored up for the righteous.

Papa continued, "It is interesting if you think about it, that the principle is to leave the inheritance to the grandchildren, rather than to the children. Most people, if they leave an inheritance at all, leave such only to their children at their death. However, when do people most need the help of an inheritance from past generations, in their twenties, when they are just starting out, or in their sixties, when their parents are eighty or ninety and will most likely pass on?"

Answering his own question, Papa replied, "Obviously when they are young and just starting out. So I believe that this is why the Proverb directs us to budget money to help and leave an inheritance for our children's children. Our family has done such for several generations. Isaac was not in need of financial help from his grandparents in his early twenties because he was such a quick learner. However, several of his cousins were."

"For example, my brother, Isaac's uncle, has three children. When each of these three children was married in their twenties, they each started out living in an apartment and began developing their careers. However, when it came time for them to buy a house, none of them went to a bank to take out a thirty-year mortgage. Their parents and grandparents had anticipated the coming need several decades ago and had preserved the money in their Savings jar to purchase each of their grandchildren a house for cash. Thus the family effectively became the bank for each succeeding generation. Because each son and daughter had learned in their family culture these same five financial secrets that I have taught Isaac, they each agreed to limit their spending, and invest in paying off the loan for their house in a maximum of ten years, rather than the thirty years that many people take."

"You see," continued Papa, "anyone could pay off a house with a standard income in ten years. The reason most don't is that they have never been taught the five secrets of wealth. Instead, they have grown up in a culture that has taught them to put all their money in one jar, have no vision, or reason to pay off the house, spend all their money on depreciating items rather than multiplying assets, and have no concept of economic cycles, so they invest in the wrong things at the wrong times, and take no practical steps toward financial blessing of future generations."

> Anyone could pay off a house with a standard income in ten years.

"Wow!" declared Bill and Sue simultaneously. "You just described our lives up 'til now. I would love to be able to do what you described for our children and grandchildren, but I have no idea how to get out of the financial trap we are in at the present moment," said Bill.

"I understand," said Papa. "Most people are paralyzed through focusing on what they don't have and what they can't do. The only way out of this trap is to take some proactive steps to change focus, change your inner attitudes and values. Let me suggest some practical tools you can work with right now to help you accomplish this.

These tools were developed some friends, Craig and Jan Hill, who have become very close to us over the last few years. You can access these tools through a charitable organization Craig and Jan have set up to help people who are in the place where they want to change and move forward in their personal and financial life, but don't know how. This organization is called Family Foundations International. Let me suggest three critical tools that will help you right now. Just a minute."

Papa disappeared, and reappeared presently with his laptop opened to the web site: *www.familyfoundations.com.* Let me make a list for you of the three resources I would recommend for you to get immediately.

- Wealth, Riches and Money[1], a book by Craig Hill and Earl Pitts

- The GOODPLAN[2], a DVD series by Craig Hill

- Financial Foundations, a weekend encounter taught by Craig Hill

"The first tool, the book *"Wealth, Riches and Money,"* will give you the initial foundation you need to begin to change your thinking and values to embrace and implement the five secrets we have talked about."

"*The GOODPLAN* video series," continued Papa, "is a play on words explaining the principle of Proverbs 13:22, 'a GOOD man leaves an inheritance for his children's children.' "GOOD" is an acronym for the phrase *"GET OUT OF DEBT."* In this video series, Craig gives you biblical teaching and a step by step practical plan how you can systematically eliminate all of your current debt, and leave a significant inheritance to help your grandchildren, thus qualifying yourself scripturally to be a 'good man.' It comes with an Excel spreadsheet for you to work weekly with your personal finances."

Several years ago, when we first saw this video series, it confirmed things that we had known and practiced in our family and community literally for generations, but we had never given language and teaching to what we were doing. When we saw this video series, it gave us an even more specific plan to ensure that no one in future generations in our family would ever need to

---

[1] Hill, Craig and Pitts, Earl, *Wealth, Riches and Money*, (Littleton, CO, Family Foundations International, 2001)

[2] Hill, Craig *The GOODPLAN*, (Littleton, CO, Family Foundations International, 2007)

take a mortgage from a bank to buy a house. I'll explain in a few minutes exactly what we have set up in our family for generational blessing."

"Then the weekend experience, *Financial Foundations* is truly a life-changing encounter with the Holy Spirit of God. When we went through this encounter several years ago, we were confronted with so many lies deep inside that were affecting our marriage relationship, our spending habits, our discernment in investing, and our ability to use the financial resources available to us to fulfill God's purpose for our lives."

"You know," said Isaac's mom, as she walked into the living room to join the conversation, "I still can't explain it, but somehow through that encounter, God supernaturally changed values and emotions deep inside both of us. Isaac, the way your father treated me, especially regarding our decisions about usage of our money was radically differently after that weekend. Something dramatically changed in him, and it seemed to me that for the first time in our married life we were on the same page regarding our finances."

"Well, something radically changed after that weekend in you too, Ketsele," interjected Papa. "But you are right, I would say that it was that *Financial Foundations* weekend encounter that really set us free to make money our servant to accomplish God's purpose through us, rather than us feeling like we were servants, or really slaves to our money."

"Man, do we need that in our marriage and lives," said Bill, with Sue heartily nodding her head in affirmation."

"Let's order the book and the DVD series for you tonight. We can look online and find out where and when will be the next *Financial Foundations* weekend that you can attend," said Papa.

"Great," said Bill, eagerly.

After they finished ordering the book and DVD series online and registering Bill and Sue for an upcoming *Financial Foundations* weekend, Papa continued, "I mentioned earlier that we had developed a very specific plan for generational blessing in our family. Isaac's mother and I had to determine what God wanted us to give unconditionally to our children just because they were our children, and what we were to give based on their embracing the values and fulfilling the goals we had. After several weeks of prayer, we determined that we would provide each of our children with a house to live in based solely on their relationship as sons and daughters. We would then invest additional resources in them based on their alignment with our spiritual and business goals and objectives."

Papa continued, "We had originally gotten this idea from the friendship we had with an Arab family living in the Galilee region of Israel. Youseff had originally built a large house with a flat roof, and had the vision of building additional stories on top of his original house to provide an apartment for each of his three sons when they married. As his sons grew up and married, Youseff did exactly that."

"So having seen our friend Youseff provide an apartment for each of his sons, we also felt that we wanted to provide a house for each of our three children. After watching the *GOODPLAN* video series, we got an idea of how we could set up a perpetual fund to provide houses for our grandchildren and all future generations. We prayed and felt impressed from God that we were not to simply give each child a house without any accountability. Instead we were to pursue a plan similar to the one presented in the *GOODPLAN*. We were to lend each married child the money at no interest to buy a house. They were then to pay the loan back over ten years."

"The money would not be paid back to us personally, but rather into a trust, the funds of which would be invested for multiplication. Then some twenty to twenty five years later, when our children's children were grown, married and ready to purchase a house there would be plenty of money in the fund to buy each of our grandchildren a house for cash. In this way, I would then qualify myself as "a good man," providing an inheritance for our children's children. We would also help all future generations in our family opt out of the financial system of debt slavery."

"The grandchildren would then make monthly payments into the trust, thus paying off their houses also in a maximum of ten years. In this way, we would have set up a perpetual fund to provide houses for our children's children and all succeeding generations. In the *GOODPLAN* video series we learned that if we followed this plan for just four generations, under the specified parameters, which are not unusual or abnormal, any family trust could end up with as much as fifty million dollars available to purchase houses for great grandchildren. So this is exactly what we have initiated in our family."

"That sounds like an incredible plan," remarked Bill. "I can't wait to get the *GOODPLAN* videos and see them myself. But what happens if one of your children defaults on their payments to the family trust?"

Papa answered, "I clearly explained to each of our children that if they ever missed a payment, they were not cheating us, but rather were stealing from their own children. The money is not going back to us, but rather into a fund to purchase houses for their own children. As a result, neither of them has ever missed a payment. So this has worked very well so far for us."

Sue then asked Isaac, "So what have you done, Isaac, regarding your children? I know that they are still young. But how are you making preparations for them?"

Isaac replied, "Actually, since we did not have a monthly payment to make for our own house, as I bought it for cash, Rachael and I began putting into our Savings jar the same amount we would have paid for our house each month. So for almost ten years we have been saving and slowly multiplying the money in that account to prepare to purchase a house for each of our children. We will easily have more than enough in that jar by the time our children are married and ready to buy a house."

Papa then turned to Isaac and Rachael and said, "We have never told you this before, but since you did not need our money to buy a house, because you had your own, we have set aside in a special account the amount of money we would have given you to purchase a house. We are slowly multiplying that money and have dedicated it to buy houses for your children, our grandchildren."

"Papa," exclaimed Isaac, "that's incredibly awesome! It looks like we may have too much money in the jar for houses for our children. If we do, we would love to be able to give more to help undernourished children, and to fund more orphanages in other developing countries around the world."

Rachael was visibly touched and just sat next to Isaac in silence, quietly weeping in response to the love and grace shown by Isaac's parents toward her and her children.

Bill could hardly believe his ears. This type of relationship between parents and adult children was completely foreign to him. Bill told the group, "This is incredible! I can't in a million years ever imagine my father saying such a thing to me. All he has told me for my entire life, especially as I have come into adulthood was that I shouldn't expect any help from him. He said, 'Nobody helped me when I was your age. I had to learn to stand on my own two feet. You need to make it on your own and become a man.' My father had no concept of generational blessing. Obviously his father, my grandfather, had the same attitude toward him."

> I also believe that God intended for each succeeding generation to excel beyond the past generation in every area of life

"I know that many families have this attitude," said Papa. "I suppose because of external persecution, our families have had to learn to stick together and to help each succeeding generation. But I also believe that God intended for each succeeding generation to excel beyond the past generation in every area of life. I believe that this is why Proverbs 13:22 talks about this 'good man' principle."

The three couples continued their conversation a little longer. Bill and Sue thanked Isaac's parents profusely for spending the evening with them. As they went out the door, Bill asked if they could meet again after they had read the book, watched the video series, and experienced the *Financial Foundations* weekend. Isaac's father graciously said that he'd be happy to meet with them again to talk about their next practical steps after they had done their homework."

While Bill and Sue did accomplish these practical steps and did have a couple more meetings with Isaac's father, unfortunately they were just not able to bring themselves to sell their house and rental house for a thirty percent loss. As a result, they eventually lost both houses to the bank in foreclosure a year later when Bill's company downsized and he lost his job. Ironically, the majority stockholder in the bank that held the mortgage on Bill and Sue's house was one of Isaac's uncles.

Secret Number 5: Plan to leave an inheritance to your children's children. Design and implement a strategy to ensure that neither your grandchildren nor any future generations in your family will ever need to borrow money from a bank and pay interest for a house.

Reflection

1. What preparations have you made to be "a good man" and leave an inheritance to your children's children?

2. In what areas has your life until now looked more like the path Bill and Sue took, and in what areas does it look more like the life Isaac and Rachael built?

3. What plans do you have to read the book, *Wealth, Riches and Money*, or watch the *GOODPLAN DVD* series, or attend a

Financial Foundations weekend seminar to move toward implementing the five wealth secrets in your life and family?

4. What practical steps can you take today to begin to leave an inheritance to your children's children?

CHAPTER 7

CONCLUSION

In our present time, many people find themselves, like Bill and Sue, already drowning in large amounts of debt. This can seem overwhelming, and very discouraging. If this is your case, take courage, as God is for you, and if you apply these five secrets to your life, you'll be shocked at how quickly your external circumstances can turn around. We have seen so many times that as you take small, simple, natural steps, you can expect God to meet you with large supernatural steps. As Isaac's father explained in an earlier chapter, one of the favorite strategies of the devil is to keep you focused on what you don't have and what you can't do. The key to actually changing your financial experience in life is to change your focus from what you don't have, to what you do have.

The ninety-six percent believe that their problem consists of not making enough money (what they don't have). The four percent realize that there is no problem. Their only challenge is to learn how to properly manage and multiply the money they do have. Therefore, your first step is to change this fundamental paradigm. Your problem is not the amount of money you have available! Instead, **the challenge before you is to choose to utilize the money you have in a different manner.** If you will make that paradigm shift, and then begin to systematically implement these five secrets, you will find your financial life improving more rapidly than you could have ever imagined. So the key is to get started with the actual implementation of these five principles, beginning from where you are, and implementing them sequentially, one at a time.

Before you start working on the five secrets, I highly suggest that you read the book *Wealth, Riches, and Money*[1] by Craig Hill and Earl Pitts. If you are in debt, I suggest that you also order the video series, *The GOODPLAN*[2], which will give you foundational Bible teaching and a practical plan to rapidly eliminate your debt. Please also check the website to see when the next *Financial Foundations* weekend experience will take place in a location near you. These materials can be ordered from the website: www.familyfoundations.com

In conclusion, let's briefly review and talk about some specific steps you can take to implement the five secrets.

Place your money in five jars.

Let's first talk about what the jars actually are for adults. Like Isaac's father, in our family, Jan and I literally used physical jars when our children were young in order to teach them this principle. As adults, we have used separate bank accounts as jars. Some people have segregated their funds in separate computer software accounts, but left the money physically in the same bank account. I believe that this presents a greater temptation to violate the allocations to each jar.

If you have not kept your money in "jars" before, I suggest that you start with five literally separate bank accounts. Most

---

[1] Hill, Craig, and Pitts, Earl, *Wealth, Riches and Money*, (Littleton, CO, Family Foundations International, Littleton, 2001)

[2] Hill, Craig, *The GOODPLAN*, (Littleton, CO, Family Foundations International, Littleton, 2007)

banks are happy to open new accounts for you and won't charge you anything for keeping money in separate accounts. This way, when you look in your Spending account, you will never see mixed in with it money allocated for other purposes, and become tempted to overspend. The bank we use allows us to set up automatic transfers between accounts, which makes the allocation to the jars very simple. It is thus possible to set up automatic transfers to distribute the appropriate amounts to the appropriate jars each time one receives income in the master account.

If you are married, I suggest that you pray together as a couple about the percentages of your income that you allocate to each jar. In the beginning this may be quite difficult if you have become accustomed to spending 100% of all your money each month, but it is important that you start with something in each jar, even if it is a very small amount. God can multiply even small numbers by large multiplication factors. However, remember that even a large factor multiplied by zero is still zero. Below is an example of a potential allocation a family might use to start with.

- The Lord's Tithe: 10%
- Offerings: 3%
- Savings: 3%
- Investment: 4%
- Spending: 80%

Some couples may look at an allocation such as that above and ask, "How could we ever reduce our spending to 80% of our income? We're perishing now utilizing 100% of our income." The answer would be to sell some depreciating items upon which monthly payments are due, and reduce lifestyle to fit the available cash flow based on the vision. Remember Papa's friend Mr. Tran from chapter one? He lived a reduced lifestyle for the sake of his vision. What is your vision? Is it clear and worthy of a present lifestyle change to be fulfilled? This leads us to the second secret.

Focus on Vision.

If you are married, pray together as a couple (if single, pray individually) to clarify your calling and vision. Many people have fallen into the trap of working for money. Instead, begin working for vision, and press money into service to work for you in fulfillment of your vision. If this is your case, I encourage you to spend some time in prayer determining what the true vision in your heart is.

Create a written vision statement that answers these two questions: 1. What did God create me to do? 2. What do I love to do? The answers to these two questions will probably lead you to a clear written vision statement. Once you have a clear vision, then spend some more time in prayer seeking God for a focused financial plan that will accommodate the fulfillment of that vision.

Part 1- Invest only in things that multiply.

If you have allowed yourself to take on any debt, your first goal is to eliminate that debt. Again, I suggest investing in the video series *The GOODPLAN*[3] to help eliminate your debt. Money you pay in interest will never multiply, but will only deplete your financial resources and cause you to be a slave to lenders. Eliminate all debt as a first priority.

Secondly, begin to accumulate money in your 'Investment' jar for the purpose of investing in things that multiply. Most people do not know how to find investments that actually multiply. Perhaps you don't have a father like Isaac did, who is already one of the four percent thinkers. One of the best suggestions I can give you is to ask God to lead you to a mentor, who has already

---

[3] *Ibid.*

learned this secret and is already skilled in this area. Receiving counsel and help from such a person is the most effective and fastest way to learn how to invest in things that truly multiply.

Part 2- If you are called to lead and grow an organization, invest in people who are faithful, and are multipliers.

A leader must determine to identify and invest in faithful multipliers in all endeavors of your life, whether they are spiritual, financial or relational. If this is your calling, start by identifying the areas of life in which you have spent your time, energy and money with people who may be your friends but are not multipliers. Reassess the investment of your resources and pray about reallocating resources away from the unproductive or unfaithful to the faithful, productive, multipliers.

This doesn't mean that you spend no time, energy or money on those who don't multiply. I suggest that you do spend resources on those who are not multipliers, but those resources should come from a different jar. It comes from the 'Offerings' jar, not from the 'Investment' jar of time, money, or energy. The Bible directed the farmers in ancient Israel to leave the corners of the field unharvested for the poor to come and glean. These farmers did indeed give grain to the poor, who were not productive multipliers. However, these farmers did not invest the majority of their time or resource with the non-productive, and they had no expectation of return from those to whom they gave the gleanings. I suggest that you do the same.

While it is right and wise to give "alms" to the non-multipliers, I suggest that you spend time, money and energy from your 'Investment' jar with people who prove to be faithful, productive, multipliers. Remember that the way to determine who is a faithful multiplier is to give many people "minas" or opportunities to respond to a challenge by a particular accountability date. Watch what each does, and invest in those who are faithful to fulfill the assignment and go beyond what was assigned to multiply to others.

The 96% rarely, if ever qualify others by giving minas, but instead simply invest in non-multipliers with an expectation that they will somehow, eventually multiply. This creates disappointment and frustration in the one investing and a large strain and tension in the relationship. It is so much less stressful to qualify through minas and only invest in faithful multipliers. You'll be amazed at the change in desired results and reduction of frustration when you shift from investing the majority of your time, money, and energy in non-multipliers to investing in faithful multipliers.

Understand, anticipate, and prepare for a cyclical economy.

Take stock of the current phase of the economic cycle, particularly as it pertains to markets that affect you, your industry, your company, or your personal life. Don't assume that what always has been in your lifetime will continue to be.

Don't take economic or financial advice only from people who have a vested interest in selling you products or services from which they make a living. Most financial planners and investment counselors in the financial services industry make a living by selling securities and investments. Receiving financial or economic advice from such people is like receiving counsel on the potential purchase of an automobile from a salesman at a car dealership. On what day will he tell you that it is a bad day to buy a car from his dealership, and you should wait until later, or not buy a car at all? Obviously, never!

Seek objective advice on the current economic cycle from non-biased sources. Determine whether the overall economy, in general and the specific sectors that affect your life, are in the expanding part of the cycle, or the contracting part of the cycle. Once you have some understanding of the current phase of the economic cycle in your nation, and can anticipate the next coming phase, then spend some time with the Lord to determine a plan to prosper in that next phase of the economy.

Plan to leave an inheritance to your grandchildren.

I suggest that you assess your current plans to help your grandchildren and leave a multigenerational inheritance. Pray together as a couple (or individually if single) as to what God's plan might be for you to bless future generations financially. Again, I might suggest *The GOODPLAN* video series as an excellent tool to help you determine how to deliver your grandchildren from the current financial system of debt slavery to lenders. We have done this in our family personally and have seen many others make significant progress toward that end. It really is possible to design and implement a strategy that insures that neither your grandchildren nor any future generations in your family will ever need to borrow money from a bank and pay interest for a house. I encourage you to pray about designing and implementing a plan in your family to qualify yourself as a "good man" by leaving an inheritance to your children's children (Proverbs 13:22).

It is important to note in conclusion that these five secrets must be implemented sequentially. It is not effective to try to implement secret number four or five, when the first three are not yet intact. Start with the concept of managing your money in jars. Just this one change may produce some dramatic results in and of itself. Once you are comfortable managing your money in jars and this is working effectively, move on to seeking God to establish a clear vision.

As you move through each step sequentially, you'll be surprised how this prepares you for the next step. Before you know it, you will be one of the wealthy four percent sharing the secrets God has shown you with others whom you are mentoring. It is my prayer for you, as Solomon prayed when he became king, that you may seek God with all your heart for the wisdom and knowledge necessary to fulfill in entirety your God-given calling and destiny. Regarding your stewardship of the resource God has placed in your hand, may you be found to be a faithful multiplier. Upon His return, may you be one to whom the Lord would say, "Well done good and faithful servant. Because you have been faithful over a very little thing, be in authority over ten cities!"

In Summary:

The ninety-six percent tend to:

- Use **No Jars**

- Have **No Vision**

- Invest in **No Multiplication**

- Have **No Awareness** of, or **Preparation for, Economic Cycles**

- Pursue **No systematic plan for Generational Blessing**

In order to move from the thinking of the 96% to the thinking of the wealthy 4%, you must embrace and engraft internally these five secrets.

Secret Number 1: **Place your money in five jars, and allocate a percentage to each jar. Voluntarily limit your spending to the percentage allocated to the Spending jar, and never rob the money in one jar to fund an activity in another jar (especially the spending jar).**

Secret Number 2: **Focus on vision not on provision. Discover your purpose and calling from God. Choose your career or profession according to calling not according to money. Then pursue your calling and** vision with all your heart and expect provision to naturally follow vision.

Secret Number 3 Part 1: Invest only in things that multiply. Never borrow money to purchase a depreciating asset, or to invest in something that doesn't increase the value of the asset or cash flow significantly more than the cost of the interest you must pay to borrow the money. Make sure to have only one Master, God, in your financial life. Live a lifestyle of meekness, and walk with margins in the significant areas of your life.

Secret Number 3 Part 2: As a leader, invest money, time and energy in people who are faithful and are multipliers. Give specific qualification tests (minas) to identify faithful multipliers. Then invest in these faithful multipliers, and do not invest major time, money, or energy in those who fail the test or don't respond to the opportunity given.

Secret Number 4: Understand that the economy is cyclical, not linear. Therefore, always anticipate and prepare for the next phase of the economic cycle. Learn how to prosper equally when the economy is contracting as you do when the economy is expanding.

Secret Number 5: Plan to leave an inheritance to your children's children. Design and implement a strategy to insure that neither your grandchildren nor any future generations in your family will ever need to borrow money from a bank and pay interest for a house.

Reflection

1. Are you one who has believed that your financial problem consisted of not making enough money? If so, what do you now understand to be the primary crux of your financial difficulty?

2. In what areas of your life have you been focused on what you don't have and what you can't do, and what is your plan to change that?

3. Which of the Five Wealth Secrets have you already implemented at least partially in your life? Which ones do you still need to work on, and what is your plan to do so?

4. What is the greatest current need for prayer in your life at this moment?

5. What is the greatest current need for prayer specifically pertaining to finances in your life at this time?

APPENDIX

About the Author

Craig Hill and his wife, Jan, live near Denver, Colorado, U.S.A. Craig and Jan give senior leadership to Family Foundations International (FFI). FFI is a non-profit Christian ministry through which life-changing seminars are conducted in many nations of the world. Craig has written several books, including his best seller, *The Ancient Paths*.

Through his past experience in business, missions, counseling and pastoral ministry, God has given Craig unique insight into marriage, family, financial and interpersonal relationships. This has resulted in his ability to identify for many people, root causes of relational conflict, compulsive habits, low self-esteem, workaholism, lack of financial provision and other undesirable life patterns, which are repeated from one generation to the next.

By interweaving personal stories with biblical truths, God has anointed Craig to pierce through the veil of the mind to minister to the depths of the heart, resulting in authentic life change for many.

& seminars courses

www.familyfoundations.com

Family Foundations International

Embracing God's Ancient Paths of Blessing–

An Experience of the Heart You'll Never Forget!

Family Foundations (FFI) is a non-profit Christian ministry, based out of Colorado, USA. FFI provides seminars and other tools through local churches and businesses in many countries around the world. Craig & Jan Hill are the founders of FFI.

The Ancient Paths Seminars give solid biblical principles, and Craig Hill's moving examples open the heart for participants to receive truth and rest for their souls. The intent of the teaching is not just for information, but to touch the heart. This often exposes hidden areas of woundedness that have occurred in the participant's life. The small group times allow participants to seek and receive God's powerful truth and light in these areas.

For a schedule of seminars or to locate the FFI office nearest you, go to www.familyfoundations.com. Seminars are available through FFI Seminar Coordinators. Courses are available for purchase.

SEMINARS

An Ancient Paths Seminar: EMPOWERING RELATIONSHIPS

Empowering Relationships is a teaching and small group seminar highlighting life's relationships with God, self and others. This 12-hour seminar includes the following topics:

- Relational versus Topical Communication
- Winning the Battle Over Destructive Attitudes, Habits and Behavior
- Removing Roots That Damage or Destroy Relationships
- Understanding and Breaking eight Negative Adult Life Patterns

An Ancient Paths Seminar: BLESSING GENERATIONS

Blessing Generations is a teaching and small group seminar on the power of blessing in seven critical times in life. In this 12-hour seminar, participants learn and experience the power of the blessing as the single most important factor that empowers people to prosper. Come, learn and apply the blessing in your life. Topics include

- Seven Critical Times of Blessing in Our Lives
- Consequences of the Lack of Blessing
- Impartation of the Father's Blessing
- The Power Behind Your Name

THE ANCIENT PATHS SEMINAR

The Ancient Paths Seminar is the original 16-hour seminar including the topics of both Empowering Relationships and Blessing Generations Seminars in a condensed format.

An Ancient Paths Seminar: COVENANT MARRIAGE (Covenant Marriage Retreat)

Married couples come to understand God's heart for their marriage, the true meaning of covenant and the power of a covenant commitment!

Learn how to add intimacy and unity as a couple and how to divorce-proof your marriage. The weekend ends in a covenant vows renewal ceremony where many couples realize for the first time the power of the covenant words in the vows they speak, sealing their marriage for life. Topics include:

- Communication in Marriage
- How to divorce-proof your marriage
- Understanding God's heart, His perfect way, for your marriage
- Why the Biblical view on blood covenant and the threshold covenant are critical to your marriage
- How marriage and covenant reflect the image of God

An Ancient Paths Seminar: OVERCOMING ANGER

Overcoming Anger is a seminar that presents practical, biblically based reasons for anger and solutions to overcome anger and other compulsive habits in people's lives. Topics include:

- The Anger Cycle
- Why do I do what I don't want to do?
- Identifying the real source of anger and frustration
- Removing the power of people and circumstances to control my life

- Three key steps to overcoming anger

An Ancient Paths Seminar: TRANSFORMING HEARTS

This is a follow-up (level 2) seminar, which may be attended following any seminar with small group ministry. Topics include:

- The authority of the believer
- Freedom from shame
- Softening the hardened heart
- Refocus on who I am in Christ

An Ancient Paths Seminar: FINANCIAL FOUNDATIONS

This seminar (and its predecessor named "Financial Success) is different from many Christian finance seminars. The teaching does not feature merely "practical" information on finances, but follows Craig Hill's anointed understanding of God's Word in teaching finances from a biblical and heart perspective (Matt. 6:21). Topics include:

- Discover the difference between wealth, riches and money
- What is "Mammon?"
- Learn a systemized guide to getting out of debt
- Learn five scriptural uses of money
- Learn how to release God's blessing in finances

An Ancient Paths Seminar: THE QUESTION

This is an exciting and life-changing teaching and audio/video presentation designed especially for young men and young women but found to open hearts of men and women of all ages. The Question (a 12-hour event) includes thought provoking teaching on video and sharing, prayer and Holy Spirit-led ministry to the heart in small groups. There are two separate versions of The Question, one for women and one for men. Topics include:

- Who have I allowed to answer that question for me?
- What difference do my actions today make?
- How should I relate to the opposite gender
- How will I know when I meet the right person who is my future spouse?

Training for Ministry

FFI's Training is an intensive time of teaching leaders and potential leaders how to identify problems and allow the Holy Spirit to guide in effective prayer ministry through small groups. Prerequisite: You must have completed at least one Family Foundations seminar. Topics include:

- Authority and Leadership
- Philosophy of Ministry
- Process of Ministry
- Ministering to Shame
- Steps of Blessing
- Identifying Strongholds

COURSES

COMMUNICATION IN MARRIAGE: *Renewing the Bond of Love*

This eight-week course, which can be purchased and conducted at the local level, is intended for a small group of married couples with a leader couple. Topics include:

- Why women criticize/accuse, and men don't listen/care

- Why have we lost the feeling of romantic love and how can we regain it?

- Learn to identify and meet the five top priority desires of your spouse

- Emotional cycles and key differences in how men and women cope with stress

- Three steps necessary to solve arguments and resolve conflict

- Conquering the single greatest hindrance to fulfillment in marriage

COURTSHIP: *God's Ancient Path to Romance and Marriage*

Courtship is a 10-week video-based study in courtship versus dating for parents and teens. This material, which can be purchased and conducted at the local level, is designed for a small group (4-5 families) of parents and young people to join together to learn and work through the topic of courtship. The goal of the course is for parents and children to have a thorough understanding of the dangerous implications of dating (the world's system) in order to come into agreement about partnering for the identification of God's choice for the son/daughter's spouse. Topics include:

- God's Plan for Romance

- Courtship vs. Dating

- Standards for Relationships

- The Door to a Young Person's Heart

- Root Causes of Teenage Rebellion

- Eight character qualities to look for in a potential spouse

- Seven Phases of a Godly Courtship

WWW.FAMILYFOUNDATIONS.COM